# CLASSIC MOUNTAIN SCRAMBLES
# IN ENGLAND AND WALES

Graham Thompson has been walking and climbing on Britain's mountains for 15 years. He lived in the Lake District for a number of years and has worked as a freelance writer, photographer and climbing instructor. He is the staff writer and photographer for *Trail Walker* magazine.

*Classic*

# MOUNTAIN SCRAMBLES in ENGLAND and WALES

## Graham Thompson

MAINSTREAM
PUBLISHING

EDINBURGH AND LONDON

First published in Great Britain in 1994 by
MAINSTREAM PUBLISHING COMPANY (EDINBURGH) LTD
7 Albany Street
Edinburgh EH1 3UG

Reprinted 1997

ISBN 1 85158 610 5

A catalogue record for this book is available from the British Library

Photography by Graham Thompson
Cover design by James Hutcheson

Typeset in Plantin by Servis Filmsetting
Printed and bound in Great Britain by Butler and Tanner Ltd, Frome

# WARNING!

## SCRAMBLING CAN BE DANGEROUS

## FOLLOW THE SCRAMBLER'S CODE

* Read and fully understand the introductory and technical notes in this guidebook before attempting any of the scrambles described.
* Be aware of the dangers associated with scrambling.
* Do not underestimate the seriousness and difficulty of a scramble.
* Be cautious and do not be afraid to avoid a scramble if conditions make the expedition unsafe.
* Keep well within your limits.
* Learn how to cope with slippery and loose rock.
* Avoid scrambles in wet or damp conditions.
* A safety rope must be carried by a party of scramblers.
* The only relatively safe way to climb grade 2 or 3 scrambles is when roped up using belays and running belays.
* Unroped scramblers must not slip.
* Learn how to use a rope and safety equipment from a qualified instructor.
* If children are taken on scrambles they should be roped up at all times.
* Scramblers should consider wearing a helmet.
* Expect holds to be slippery in gill scrambles. Consider using socks over footwear for a better grip.

*For Dawn, whose continual support made
it possible to complete this book*

# CONTENTS

# ACKNOWLEDGMENTS

This book could not have been produced without the assistance of many people. Jeremy Ashcroft has been particularly helpful in suggesting routes and the style of the maps, and has guided me through the minefield of publishing.

Thanks also to Paddy Dillon for route suggestions. Terry Marsh has given me advice on the correct spelling of Welsh place-names. I must also thank R.B. Evans and Steve Ashton, whose scrambling guidebooks have provided the starting point for many of my scrambling explorations. For the same reason, thanks also to Keith Nelson and David Ogle of *Trail Walker* magazine who began publishing scrambling routes on a regular basis.

Thanks to Martin Allen, Simon Morley, John Newsome, Simon Holmes, Tony Remmer, Richard Hardy, Guy Harrup and Sue Hooper for accompanying me on scrambles and providing patient models for photography. Additional thanks to anyone else who appears in a photograph but has not been mentioned here by name.

Thanks to Matthew Roberts and Tom Bailey who printed all the black and white photographs. I would also like to thank Reg and Gwen Gibson for their hospitality during regular weekend trips to Wales.

Finally, special thanks to Dawn Gibson for proof-reading, accompanying me on routes, and providing continual support throughout this project.

*Scrambling over the top of Harrow Buttress, Grey Crags*

# INTRODUCTION

## What is Scrambling?

The broad grey area between simple walking and technical climbing is described as scrambling. In its simplest form, scrambling begins when a walker places a hand on the rock to negotiate a tricky step. At the top of the scale, scrambling involves exposed moves, with big holds on steep rock where a slip may be fatal.

Many of the classic scrambles have been climbed since Victorian times. As the standard of climbing improved, the scrambles were soon forgotten as climbers concentrated on progressively harder rock-climbs. Today, rock-climbing guidebooks generally only refer to routes that border on pure rock-climbs. Walking guides, on the other hand, step carefully and only give information on the most well-worn and easy classics. Recently, more guides have started to appear that are dedicated to scrambling as a sport in itself. This book attempts to cover the very best scrambling routes in both England and Wales, from the easiest to the hardest and the popular to the little known.

Scramblers may be regarded as strange beasts. They revel in exposed situations, often without a rope to be seen. A rope will often be carried in the rucksack, ready for use should a section become too dangerous. Their adventures sometimes take them on to loose rock and directly up roaring waterfalls.

Any adventurous sport is dangerous – otherwise many adventurous souls wouldn't try it. While the adventure is clear, the safety aspects of scrambling should not be overlooked or taken lightly. There is no doubt that unroped scrambling in exposed situations is potentially the most dangerous form of mountaineering. It is probably fair to say that the unroped scrambler in such a situation is someone who is lucky to be alive.

Make no mistake, the only relatively safe way to climb grade 2 or 3 scrambles is when roped up using belays and running belays. It is also essential that the use of the rope is coupled with a wide experience in mountaineering. A leader must have a cautious approach and be able to assess the conditions of the rock, the ability of the party and the difficulty of the terrain, and must not be afraid to retreat should conditions become unsafe.

## Types of Scramble

Within the broad spectrum of scrambling there are various types of scrambles, from open, airy ridge traverses to dark, dank gill scrambles. Each type of scramble has its own form of excitement, adventure and associated dangers.

### Gill Scrambles

Many of the best scrambles in England are to be found in the gills of the Lake District. These often provide a direct route from the valley floor to the fell tops.

It is an unwritten rule that, when gill scrambling, the hardest route is followed as near as possible to the waterline. It is therefore logical to climb gills when the water level is low, thus ensuring that visible, water-washed rocks can be used during the ascent. Waterproof clothing is often advisable as it may be necessary to pass very close or even through a waterfall. In any conditions, it is fair to assume that scramblers will get at least their legs wet.

The rock in gills is often wet and slippery. Use socks over footwear to get a better grip. Holds need to be checked to ensure that they are adequate to overcome the most slippery rock.

After or during rain most gills should be avoided. This is not only because of the basic difficulty of climbing them; there is also the problem of the high water forcing scramblers on to the vegetated slopes of the ravine above the normal waterline. This vegetation is very fragile and considerable erosion can be caused by climbing on it rather than the rock in the stream-bed.

Scenically, gills are very beautiful places in which to search out adventure. Please be aware of how fragile this environment is and keep the disturbance to a minimum.

## Buttress Scrambles

Rock outcrops and crags form the basis of many scrambles. The route will find the best line through the rock, often with intricate route-finding challenges along the way. In some cases a series of crags will be linked together to form one continuous line of scrambling, usually directly from the valley floor to the tops of the fells. These routes sometimes have the advantage that it is possible to bypass difficult pitches or even whole crags by tracing a line around some sections. Remember, though, that leaving the scramble may also lead to more difficult terrain around the edges of the crags.

On other scrambles the route will climb one single crag from valley floor to mountain summit. These routes are obviously very serious and do not allow any easy escape. Often the only escape is to down climb the route or retreat by abseil. Both of these methods of escape are fraught with danger and a high degree of experience is required to perform them safely.

Care is required on buttress scrambles in order to check the rock carefully. It can be very difficult to judge the quality of rock, so avoid a direct pull on any rock. Loose blocks should be treated carefully at all times. Often there will be vegetation on buttress scrambles. Before pulling on any branches check that they are firmly attached to the mountain.

## Ridge Scrambles

The ridge scrambles of Crib Goch in Snowdonia and Sharp Edge in the Lake District are perhaps the most popular scrambles in the country. Although route-finding may be relatively simple, there will often be no escape except by down-climbing the ridge. The sides of the ridge may be very steep, so a slip could be serious. Rope techniques on ridges can be very difficult, so a high level of skill and experience is required to traverse a difficult ridge safely with adequate rope protection.

Ridge scrambles should be avoided in high winds.

## Route Classification

The Victorian climbing pioneers defined the difficulty of the rock-climbs they were discovering by use of the descriptive terms Easy, Moderate, Difficult and Very Difficult. As climbing standards improved, the terms Hard, Very Difficult, Severe, Very Severe, Hard Very Severe and finally Extreme were introduced. When standards rose still higher the descriptive terms were extended by the letter E to denote an Extreme grade. A number from one to nine was then added to define the level of Extremity; thus E1 is a relatively easy extreme and E9 is a very difficult extreme grade of climb.

When scrambling grades were established around ten years ago, the numerical denomination was used. The grades for scrambles most commonly used are simply Grade One, Two or Three. For extremely difficult scrambles that border on Moderate or even Difficult rock-climbs, a grade of 3S is given.

Scrambling grades may be defined as follows:

### Grade 1

A simple scramble with few route-finding difficulties. The line may be varied at will and difficult sections can be bypassed. Generally, the degree of exposure is not too great. It will usually be possible to descend the route safely and without difficulty. A rope will usually not be required.

### Grade 2

This will be longer and demand more commitment from the scrambler. There will be difficult pitches of scrambling and some skill in route-finding will be required. It will not be possible to use the route in descent. A rope may be required on some exposed sections and to aid a retreat from the scramble. The only relatively safe way to climb grade 2 routes is as a roped climb, using belays and running belays. Unroped scrambling is only for the very experienced.

### Grade 3

More serious scrambles that should only be undertaken by experienced parties. There will be short sections of simple rock-climbing up to the grade of Moderate. There will be very difficult route-finding problems. It will not be possible to use the route in descent. Dry conditions are essential. All but very experienced scramblers will require the protection of a rope along with a selection of nuts and slings. The only relatively safe way to climb grade 3 routes is as a roped climb using belays and running belays.

### Grade 3S

Particularly serious routes. A solo scrambler would be in great danger. There will be sections of Moderate grade rock-climbing. The rock may be poor or there may be long stages of considerable exposure. There may be a lack of good belays and it will be difficult to retreat from the route once started. Dry conditions are essential. These routes are only for experienced climbers and scramblers. Anyone attempting a grade 3S scramble will require a rope along with a selection of nuts and slings. The only relatively safe way to climb grade 3S routes is as a roped climb using belays and running belays.

## Scrambling Safety

It should be remembered that the grade given to a scramble describes the difficulty of the route in perfect dry summer conditions. When the rock is wet or the ambient air temperature does not allow ungloved scrambling, the routes become at least a grade more difficult. In such conditions a rope will be required on grade 1 scrambles as well as the more difficult routes. It is unadvisable to attempt scrambles in wet or damp conditions, when many routes become too hazardous to be safe.

The difficulty of a scramble is also related to your own particular experience. Less experienced walkers may be horrified by the exposure and difficulty of the moves. Experienced climbers will often take scrambles easily in their stride but they too should not underestimate the dangers and seriousness of scrambling. It is essential that all scramblers stay well within their limits.

Even though the lower grades of scrambles may be thought suitable for children, this is not advised.

Children often do not possess the fear or judgment necessary to scramble safely on their own. They must be roped up at all times and their leader must be very experienced in rope techniques.

It is essential that scramblers learn how to use a rope and have experience of the various techniques involved before venturing onto a scramble where the rope will be required. The section on rope technique at the back of this book provides some basic information. The safest way to learn rope technique is from a qualified instructor.

If a scrambler does fall, it is very likely that they will receive a head injury and, as many scrambles pass over crags where there is much loose rock, it is recommended that scramblers wear a helmet.

When there is snow or ice on the rock during winter, all scrambles become very difficult and require entirely different skills and equipment to those used in summer conditions. All routes and safety techniques described in this guide are intended and described for summer conditions.

## Selection of Routes

The routes selected for this guide concentrate on the truly classic mountain scrambles in England and Wales. To set some kind of limits on what would be included, it was decided that all the routes should provide worthwhile, long and exhilarating scrambles that lead to a mountain summit. The short scrambles that litter the valleys have therefore been excluded in preference for longer routes of more continuous interest.

The guide has been divided into areas, each covering a single or small group of mountains. Many of the most famous and classic scrambles are collected in one area and even on one particular mountain. It has therefore been unavoidable that some wonderful mountains have not been visited in this guide.

## Route Descriptions

Each route is given an introductory paragraph that describes the general style or appeal of a route. A concise fact file details some essential information that will be required before the route can be climbed. This is set out as follows:

**Grade:** The grade of 1, 2, 3 or 3S (as described above) is given for the whole route if climbed under normal dry conditions. Borderline cases are indicated by 1/2 or 2/3. It is impossible to apply any grading system rigorously and at best this can only be a rough guide.

**Quality:** All the routes have been given a quality star rating from one to three. Stars are given for factors such as length of continuous scrambling interest, quality of rock, quality of the scrambling and the location.

**Distance:** A complete round including a mountain summit has been described for each scramble. The distance refers to the approximate length of the complete round from start to finish.

**Total Ascent:** The total ascent refers to the approximate total height climbed on the round.

**OS Map:** The number of the Ordnance Survey 1:50,000 map is given. This will help in planning and is an adequate map to use on most scrambles in clear weather. However, it is recommended that the appropriate OS Outdoor Leisure (1:25,000) map is also used. These provide more detail and are preferred for accurate mountain navigation.

**Time:** The time is for completion of the whole round, including stops. For this reason and because some people walk faster or stop longer than others, a time range is given. It is inevitably only an estimate.

**Start/Finish:** This is the start and finish point for each complete scrambling round. All the routes finish at the starting point.

**Escape Routes:** Describes how an escape may be made. It may also state whether a rope would be required to effect an escape safely.

**Notes:** Any points that should be considered by a scrambler, such as recommendations to carry a rope or when the scramble should be avoided, are given here.

## Route Illustrations

All the routes are drawn at a scale of 1:50,000. These are intended as a quick reference and not as a substitute for the appropriate Ordnance Survey map. The route of each scramble is shown by heavy dashes. Some routes are also shown on crag diagrams. These indicate the general outline of the route on the crag and are given where the route is particularly difficult to find.

## Access

The routes described in this guidebook follow rights-of-way wherever possible. A scrambler should not have any problems of access. Rights of access often change, however, and scramblers should always check the situation and be prepared to use an alternative route if necessary. Remember that all the upland areas are owned by someone. If in doubt, check locally before venturing on to the hills.

## Scrambling and the Environment

This guidebook covers some of the most beautiful mountain areas in England and Wales. Concern has been expressed by conservationists regarding the damage to vegetation and the disturbance of wildlife on some scrambles, particularly those that follow the lines of gills. Many of the crags, gills and gullies in Snowdonia and the Lake District have rare plants living on them. Any removal of vegetation could be disastrous with the numbers of some plants being drastically reduced.

Many rare plants are protected by law and offenders can be prosecuted under the 1991 Wildlife and Countryside Act. Many uncommon bird species also live on the mountains where scramblers find their sport, and these can be disturbed as easily as vegetation. The same protection given to plants exists for birds. Penalties are enforceable by law.

Therefore, while on the mountains do all you can to minimise damage to the environment. A few simple actions can make all the difference. Be aware of the problems that overuse of a scramble can produce. Be prepared to sample various mountain walks and scrambles to spread the load. Leave the gill or crag as you found it by not disturbing plants and wildlife. In a gill or gully, stay down on the rocks as near to the watercourse as possible. If there is no way of scrambling near the edge of the watercourse this usually means that the water is too high or you are off route. Do not continue along the route in such conditions. Climbing up the sides of a gill or gully disturbs the delicate plant life that is too far away even for sheep to get at. If you are scrambling within your limits and the water is not too high, there will be no reason to climb up the sides of a gill, except where there is a path that is used to avoid a particular obstacle. Only climb up the sides of the gill if it is necessary for a safe escape.

To save damaging the environment stick to the intended route of a scramble and only attempt routes that are within your limits.

# ENGLAND

The main upland area of England is located to the north of the country. The Pennine backbone offers bleak moorland and rolling dales, some of which are enclosed in the Peak District and Yorkshire Dales National Parks. In the north-west of the country the Lake District National Park captures the main arena of high mountains in England. The area is small when compared with Scotland, and tiny when compared to the greater ranges of the world, but it has much to offer the tourist, walker and scrambler alike.

The Lake District National Park is the largest in Britain and covers an area of 2,243 square kilometres. It contains the highest mountains in England including four summits over the magical 3,000ft (914m). For the mountain walker there is arguably no finer place in England. The mountains are easily reached from the surrounding towns which are all in close proximity to high fells. The scenery is beautiful and intricately woven with gills and waterfalls tumbling between the crags and cliffs of the rolling fells.

For the mountain scrambler the Lake District holds the finest routes in England. The fells offer a wide variety of opportunities, from a short gill scramble to a high mountain route of over 300m in length. Nowhere else in Britain is there such variety and beauty in such a small area.

The weather is predominantly poor, with clouds hanging over the fell tops for weeks on end and seemingly never-ending drizzle or rain in the valleys. But there are good days when the skies are clear and the views from the tops extend to Scotland, Wales and the Pennines.

The fells are clustered into groups around valleys and lakes. There are ample opportunities for accommodation from a camp-site to a hotel. The main valley bases are Langdale, Coniston, Eskdale, Wasdale, Buttermere, Borrowdale, Keswick, Patterdale and Ambleside.

Outside of the Lake District there are a few other scrambles though they are not comparable to the routes selected here. At the end of this section there is a short description of other routes including some in the Howgills and Yorkshire Dales.

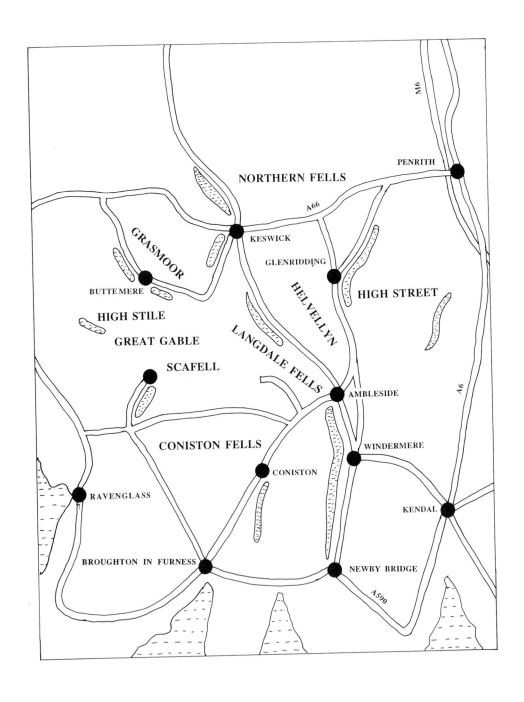

# INTRODUCTION TO THE GREAT GABLE AND PILLAR RANGE

The classic mountain pyramid shape of Great Gable forms the basis of the Lake District National Park emblem. The mountain overlooks the patchwork field system of Wasdale Head. It is on this mountain that rock-climbing in England became a recognised sport. Great Gable, along with its neighbours, Kirk Fell, Pillar and Yewbarrow, also includes much of the finest mountain walking in Lakeland. It is not surprising, then, to discover that the range also contains some of the Lake District's finest scrambles.

Great Gable has two faces. From the north, east and west it simply looks like a great massif with no classical shape. It is only from Wasdale that the fine pyramid outline of the mountain can be viewed. Maybe it was this view that led the early climbing pioneers to base themselves below its slopes at Wasdale Head to find adventurous routes on Scafell, Pillar and Gable.

Two of the routes on Great Gable, Sourmilk Gill and Gillercombe Buttress, approach the mountain from Seathwaite at the head of Borrowdale. The classic Climber's Traverse line is climbed from Wasdale Head and forms one of the finest walks and scrambles in

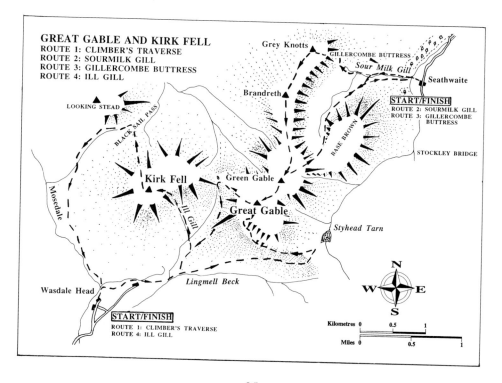

GREAT GABLE AND KIRK FELL
ROUTE 1: CLIMBER'S TRAVERSE
ROUTE 2: SOURMILK GILL
ROUTE 3: GILLERCOMBE BUTTRESS
ROUTE 4: ILL GILL

Grey Knotts
GILLERCOMBE BUTTRESS
Sour Milk Gill
Seathwaite

Brandreth

LOOKING STEAD

BLACK SAIL PASS

START/FINISH
ROUTE 2: SOURMILK GILL
ROUTE 3: GILLERCOMBE BUTTRESS

BASE BROWN

STOCKLEY BRIDGE

Mosedale

Kirk Fell

Green Gable

Great Gable

Ill Gill

Styhead Tarn

Wasdale Head

Lingmell Beck

START/FINISH
ROUTE 1: CLIMBER'S TRAVERSE
ROUTE 4: ILL GILL

N W E S

Kilometres 0    0.5    1
Miles 0    0.5    1

the country. Finally, there is the Honister approach via the steep cliffs of Honister Crag on the north face of Fleetwith Pike. This has been included under the Buttermere Fells section but provides a good approach to Gable.

To the west of Great Gable is the huge sprawling bulk of Kirk Fell. In any other arena, Kirk Fell would stand supreme, but against such a neighbour it becomes a poor second and is rarely climbed for its own sake. Kirk Fell does not have the crags or the classic climbs that Gable boasts but it does have some hidden wonders to discover. One of these is Ill Gill, a long, winding ravine up its south-eastern flank that is undoubtedly one of the finest scrambles in Lakeland.

To the west of Kirk Fell lies Pillar. Its glory is Pillar Rock which lies to the north of the mountain, overlooking Ennerdale. The rock has been scaled since climbing began with ever harder routes. But the scrambler can also enjoy this knob of rock. The Slab and Notch route leads around the eastern side of the cliffs in a tremendously exposed position overlooking the head of Ennerdale.

From Wasdale Head, Pillar forms the basis of the classic Mosedale Horseshoe walk that takes in Red Pike and Yewbarrow before descending to Wast Water. As a variation to this classic round, there is a scramble featured here on the southern slopes of Pillar via Wistow Crags. The route is set at the head of Mosedale and takes advantage of one of the few quieter corners around Wasdale.

# CLIMBER'S TRAVERSE

*The Great Napes crags, on the south-*
*ern slopes of Great Gable, are the*
*centrepiece of this masterpiece. The*
*Climber's Traverse is one of the finest*
*walks and scrambles in Britain and it*
*passes Napes Needle where the sport*
*of rock-climbing began in Britain*
*over a century ago.*

---

**Grade: 2**
**Quality: ★★★**
**Distance: 5.5km (7 miles)**
**Total Ascent: 809m (2,654ft)**
**OS Map: 89 or 90**
**Time: 5–6 hours**
**Start/Finish: Wasdale Head (GR 187088)**
**Escape Routes: Most of the dif-**
**ficult sections can be bypassed**
**via a path lower down the fell.**
**Notes: A generally well-worn**
**route. It can be difficult to**
**locate Napes Needle, especially**
**in mist. Wait for a fine day. A**
**rope should be carried.**

---

The Great Napes crags as seen from Wasdale Head are a steep band of rock surrounded by scree. It was on these crags that the modern sport of rock-climbing began in Britain.

Along the base of the crags there is an 18m pinnacle of rock standing alone from the main crag. This is Napes Needle. In 1886 Walter Parry Haskett-Smith, a Trinity College student, became the first man to climb the Needle. He made the ascent solo and without any climbing aids. Today, the route is graded Hard Very Difficult. Most of the earth and stones that jammed the cracks have been removed and the holds are very polished.

You don't need to be a climber to scale the Climber's Traverse, though. This scramble passes behind Napes Needle on a route known as Threading The Needle and then proceeds up the Sphinx Ridge and Westmorland Crags to reach the summit of Great Gable.

It is possible to begin the day from Seathwaite at the head of Borrowdale. A path leads easily from there to Sty Head. But the finer approach is from Wasdale Head, where Haskett-Smith stayed during his explorations of the Lakeland crags. From Wasdale Head the superb cone of Great Gable is also seen at its best.

Follow the path east under the grass slopes of Gavel Neese. A steady climb across the scree slopes of Gable eventually breaks out on to the grass col of Sty Head, from where the Climber's Traverse begins.

At Sty Head, turn back on yourself and pick up a path that begins to traverse along the western flank of Gable above the path that you have already climbed. The first landmark is Kern Knotts Crag. The left of the two cracks was first climbed by Owen Glynne Jones in 1879. He

*Great Gable from Scafell Pike*

used the tactic of standing on his partner's shoulders which was commonplace in the pioneering days. Today the route is graded Mild Very Severe.

The track is easy to follow as it climbs along the bed of scree across the mountain. The path crosses the red scree of Great Hell Gate and the enormous rock-face of Trophet Wall. Soon the Napes Ridges come into view and the path splits in two. The left fork stays below the scrambling and continues across the face of Gable for a messy haul up Little Hell Gate to the summit. The scrambler's route forks right towards Napes Needle, which is now visible above.

Scramble up the clear path that leads to the right and behind the Needle. The next stage is known as Threading The Needle. Climb up the groove between Napes Needle and the main crag with plenty of squeezing and shuffling. At the top there is a tiny rock cleft, between Napes Needle and Needle Ridge. The scramble now continues down the other side into Needle Gully. You are now on the west side of Napes Needle which is the view usually seen on postcards. To get the best view of Napes Needle, cross the scree chute to a narrow ledge, known as the Dress Circle.

Continue the scramble by traversing along the crags and at one point squeezing through a gap to the Sphinx Rock, the strange face-like piece of rock overlooking Wasdale. It is now possible to continue to Little Hell Gate on the other side of the Sphinx Rock. But to gain the summit of Great Gable by this approach is a poor way to end the Climber's Traverse. Instead, climb the Sphinx Ridge behind the Sphinx Rock. To gain the ridge, scramble up the gully on its right for 6m before stepping left on to the crest. This is a superb scramble in a stunning situation with good holds.

At the end of the ridge the broken rocks of Westmorland Crags come into view. The walker's route heads left to scamper up scree, then a swing to the right leads to the summit of Gable. The scrambler's route follows a faint path on the right to the base of Westmorland Crags. Reach the base of the crags where there is a shattered block above. Stay on the right of the ridge and gain the crest by climbing up a corner. The shattered ridge can then be followed. The gully on the right can be used to avoid the most difficult section across a jagged knife-edge crest. Soon the Westmorland Cairn comes into view. This marks the end of the scrambling and the summit of Great Gable is only a short walk away.

To descend, head north-west to Beck Head, then follow the path down Gavel Neese to Wasdale. For a longer round, head over Kirk Fell and descend from Black Sail Pass into Mosedale and so to Wasdale.

# SOURMILK GILL

*Sourmilk Gill is one of the most popular gill scrambles in the Lake District. It provides an adventurous route to Great Gable.*

---

**Grade:** 1/2
**Quality:** ★★★
**Distance:** 8km (5 miles)
**Total Ascent:** 770m (2,540ft)
**OS Map:** 89 or 90
**Time:** 4–5 hours
**Start/Finish:** Seathwaite (GR 235122)
**Escape Routes:** Easier paths avoid the scramble at many stages.
**Notes:** Wait for a dry spell. The route is ideally combined with a scramble over Gillercombe Buttress (Route 3).

---

Those walkers wanting a change from the route to Great Gable via Styhead Tarn from Borrowdale should investigate the high, hanging, soggy valley of Gillercombe. There is a path up the left bank of Sourmilk Gill that leads into Gillercombe from where Green and Great Gable are easily gained. Those looking for some scrambling sport, however, should take a line directly up the waterfalls of Sourmilk Gill. It is possible to escape at all times should the waters be more than just a trickle. The route dips and dives between whirlpools and waterfalls, picking the best and often wettest line to the summits.

As with most adventures from the head of Borrowdale the day begins at Seathwaite, supposedly the wettest place in England. Sourmilk Gill is clearly in view from the farm at the head of Seathwaite. Walk through the farm and take the path on the right that crosses the River Derwent via a wooden bridge. A clear path leads to the base of the waterfalls from where the scrambling can begin.

The first major fall crashes into a deep, green, swirling pool. There are a number of adventurous possibilities, but the best is to climb a series of wet boulders on the right.

A short wall provides a welcome escape from the grasp of the water from where easier scrambling continues over wet slabs. The excited spray of the water is never far away, though, and it is difficult to escape completely dry-shod.

The waterfalls gradually build in size, with each requiring a little more care to scramble safely and to escape dry. The crux of the scramble arrives with a thundering crescendo of water exploding from a cleft in the rock. There is no route directly up this flood of water. Even by inspecting its edges a drenching would be assured. The only safe escape is to join the path on the left.

The gill scramble is now over. If you are still eager for some sport then head for Gillercombe Buttress (Route 3). Otherwise join the walker's path up to Green Gable. A final pull up a badly eroded path leads to Great Gable and its magnificent views across Wasdale.

It is best to retrace your steps to Green Gable and follow the walker's path back down the banks of Sourmilk Gill.

*The main falls of Sourmilk Gill, Borrowdale*

# GILLERCOMBE BUTTRESS

*Gillercombe Buttress is a massive cliff of rock and is mainly a playground for climbers. To one side there is a route that makes the perfect continuation to a scramble up Sourmilk Gill.*

---

**Grade:** 3
**Quality:** ★★
**Distance:** 8km (5 miles)
**Total Ascent:** 770m (2,540ft)
**OS Map:** 89 or 90
**Time:** 5–6 hours
**Start/Finish:** Seathwaite (GR 235122)
**Escape Routes: Difficult to escape the route once started, although some tricky sections can be bypassed.**
**Notes: A rope and selection of nuts and slings should be taken. Avoid in the wet. Some route-finding difficulties.**

---

Gillercombe Buttress lies below Brandreth at the back of a hanging hollow. The crag has many classic rock-climbs directly up the steep front face with such names as Citizen Kane and The Wizard of Oz. The crag is marked on its right-hand side by a fan of scree. To the right of this the scramble leads over the skyline crags to the tops.

At grade 3 the route is a notch harder than the scramble up Sourmilk Gill, which is the best line of approach to this scramble. Bentley Beetham first realised this route and named it Rabbit's Trod. It has a real mountaineering flavour, with the passage of boots over the years ensuring easier route-finding. But it is still possible to stray on to difficult terrain in the central section, so take extra care with your route-finding.

Gain the hanging valley of Gillercombe either by a scramble up Sourmilk Gill or by the walker's path up its left bank. From the top of the gill a springy, soggy, bog cotton meadow leads to the base of the crags. Head to the right of the main buttress to a scree chute. Cross the scree and join the lower slabs up the right of the scree.

The scrambling is easy to start and the sport really begins as you enter the jaws of the gully. Delicate footwork is soon required to cross the slabs. If taken direct, this section proves very tricky, but there is a line of weakness: a narrow ledge that climbs further into the jaws of the gully on a rising traverse from right to left, followed by another traverse from left to right. Height is quickly gained and the seriousness of the scramble soon becomes apparent. Rope up to be safe and take your time to find the best line.

At the top of the slabs there is a terrace and the ridge arcs across the skyline to the left. The way now curves around the northern end of the buttress to gain that ridge. Scrambling along the edge takes nerve, a cool head and a breeze-free day. The safer option takes a line up the middle of the buttress on less exposed terrain.

At a wall, the rapid progress ends. A series of cracks on the left look tempting, but they are not for scramblers. Instead, escape right up a short corner. More slabs continue easily over the top of the buttress until finally blending into the fell tops of Grey Knotts and Brandreth. The height has been gained, the scrambling is over and the summits of Green Gable and Great Gable are the natural continuation of the day.

*Scrambling on Gillercombe Buttress, Brandreth*

# ILL GILL

*Ill Gill is a superb scramble that gives around 400m of continual adventure. It is set in a narrow and steep ravine. During a dry spell it is surely the finest approach to the summit of Kirk Fell.*

---

**Grade:** 3S
**Quality:** ★★★
**Distance:** 7.5km (5 miles)
**Total Ascent:** 730m (2,400ft)
**OS Map:** 89 or 90
**Time:** 4–5 hours
**Start/Finish:** **Wasdale Head (GR 186087)**
**Escape Routes:** **There are a number of places to escape the ravine, but in some locations it is easy to become trapped and an abseil descent is the only viable means of escape.**
**Notes: The route is only really feasible during a dry spell. A rope and a selection of nuts and slings should be carried in case of abseil retreat due to high water or difficulties.**

---

The great bulk of Kirk Fell is somewhat overshadowed by the more picturesque lines of Great Gable, Pillar and Scafell Pike. Many walkers would probably not notice Ill Gill on the south-eastern flanks of the mountain as they crawl up Gavel Neese *en route* for Beckhead.

Once spotted, the long, deep, narrow ravine of Ill Gill begs for attention. The route is long and best left for a dry spell when the falls are passable dry-shod. From the top of the scramble the summit of Kirk Fell is only a short walk away.

Begin the day at Wasdale Head. Follow the old trade route towards Sty Head around the base of Kirk Fell. Where the path crosses a bridge over Gable Beck turn left and begin the climb towards Beckhead. The slopes of Kirk Fell are smooth but as you gain height you will see the dark chasm of Ill Gill rising towards the sky. Traverse the grass slopes and head for the base of the gill where it joins Gable Beck above a waterfall.

The scrambling can now begin. The route follows the watercourse from bottom to top with a few escapes to avoid the most difficult pitches. It is easy to begin with as the scramble enters the depths of the gill beneath the trees, among small pools of swirling water.

The first difficult section is a 6m waterfall. This is negotiated on the right wall with good holds. A second cascade proves more difficult and an escape is possible beyond it on the right. This escape allows the scrambler to avoid the very difficult following section, which comprises a double cascade. The first fall is climbable but the second is not unless the gill is very dry. It is safest to avoid both and escape before getting trapped.

*Negotiating waterfalls near the start of Ill Gill, Kirk Fell*

Follow the top edge of the ravine and cross a rocky outcrop to a scree run. Walk down this carefully and step to the right near the bottom to avoid a steep drop into the gorge.

Small cascades continue up the ravine and provide good scrambling. A wall proves difficult. The left wall comprises soft crumbly rock and vegetation. It is difficult to climb without pulling off a hold, but a left to right traverse is the route to go for. Alternatively, leave the gill and rejoin it above the difficulties.

A rising staircase of water-washed rocks leads to a junction of two gullies. On the right there is a scree chute. Our route continues up the main ravine on the left with loose rock in its base.

The rocky scree bed leads further up the mountain then swings to the right. The water runs over a pink-veined rock step. Climb this on the right. The scrambling continues easily to where the main flow of water pours over a steep wall on the left. Climb the rocks to the left of the fall and follow the broken ridge towards the summit.

Kirk Fell is a fine place to take a break and consider the rest of the day. You are ideally placed to take in either Great Gable to the north or Pillar and the Mosedale Horseshoe to the west. But for most walkers the shorter round back to Wasdale Head via Black Sail Pass and Mosedale will be enough for the day, especially if there was a little more water in the gill than anticipated.

# SLAB AND NOTCH

*The ascent of Pillar Rock via the Slab and Notch route is one of the most famous scrambles in the Lake District.*

---

**Grade: 3**
**Quality: ★★★**
**Distance: 16.5km (10.5 miles)**
**Total Ascent: 1,190m (3,900ft)**
**OS Map: 89**
**Time: 5–7 hours**
**Start/Finish: Wasdale Head (GR 186097)**
**Escape Routes: There is no escape except by reversing the route. This is a serious scramble on a rock-climbing face.**
**Notes: The route has to be reversed in descent. Take a rope, slings and selection of nuts. Avoid the route when wet.**

---

The Slab and Notch route is one of the most popular difficult scrambles in the Lake District. It is the easiest route to the summit of Pillar Rock, which some say is the most divine, elegant and aesthetic climbing cliff in England. The cliff is nearly 300m high and is separated from Pillar mountain by a short spur. The scramble was first climbed in 1861 by the keeper of St Bees lighthouse and four friends. These days it is often used as a way down for rock-climbers.

The rock can be reached from either Ennerdale or Wasdale. But there is no access to the head of Ennerdale for vehicles, and the long walk required down the valley deters many. The finer approach is from Wasdale, unless you stay overnight at Black Sail Youth Hostel or camp wild at the head of the valley.

From Wasdale walk to Black Sail Pass via Mosedale. Swing left and head for Pillar mountain along the main path. Before a steep climb, a small cairn can be seen on the right. Beside it a path leads around to the Ennerdale side of the mountain. This is the High Level Route and is a superb walk in its own right. The path is narrow and offers stunning views down the Ennerdale valley.

After many turns and rises the path arrives at a col, with a large cairn on the right. This is Robinson's Cairn and ahead is the first view of Pillar Rock.

The table-top summit of Pillar Rock is known as High Man. To its right and slightly lower is, logically, Low Man. To the left of High Man there is a gap called Jordon's Gap and to the left of this Pisagh. The inclined slab at the start of the Slab and Notch can be clearly identified below the steep face leading to High Man and just to the right of Jordon's Gap.

The start of the scramble is reached by following the path into Pillar Cove to the left and then climbing the steep scree terrace

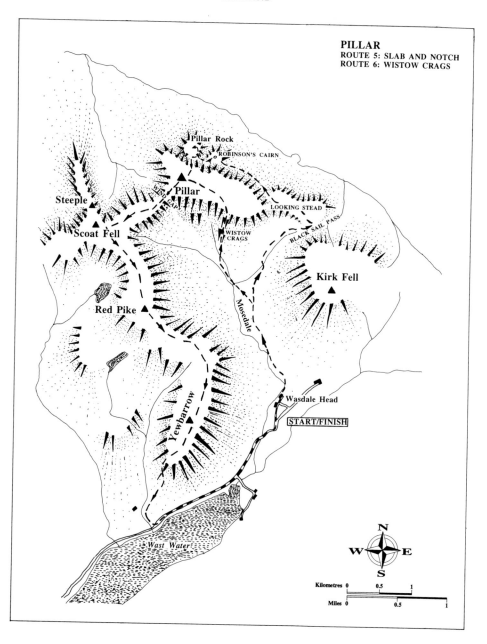

PILLAR
ROUTE 5: SLAB AND NOTCH
ROUTE 6: WISTOW CRAGS

Pillar Rock

ROBINSON'S CAIRN

Steeple

Pillar

LOOKING STEAD

Scoat Fell

WISTOW
CRAGS

BLACK SAIL PASS

Kirk Fell

Red Pike

Mosedale

Yewbarrow

Wasdale Head

START/FINISH

Wast Water

N
W E
S

Kilometres 0    0.5    1

Miles 0    0.5    1

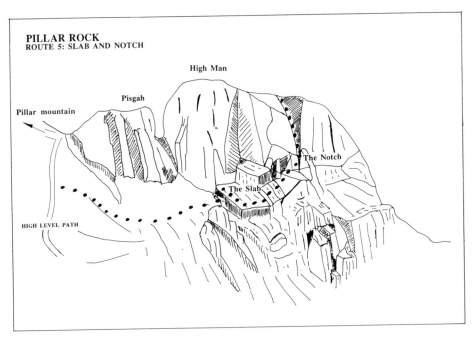

**PILLAR ROCK**
ROUTE 5: SLAB AND NOTCH

High Man

Pisgah

Pillar mountain

The Notch

The Slab

HIGH LEVEL PATH

known as the Shamrock Traverse; the rocks and crags below the terrace are called Shamrock. The titled slab of the Slab and Notch route is now clearly in view and a path can be seen leading to its base. Gaining the slab is the first tricky move. A couple of rock steps lead on to the top of it from where a bum shuffle or a controlled down-climb leads to the small grass terrace at the base of the slab. Be careful here, though, for the ground drops steeply away at the end of the slab.

Walk to the right along the terrace to a corner below the Notch, a gap on the ridge to the left of a small tower. Climb the Notch on good holds then follow another ledge right to further good holds up a ridge. An obvious track leads to a gully on the right and a short scramble leads to the summit. The summit is a fine place to take in the

view, but remember you have to get down the same way.

When Lieutenant Wilson RN of Troutbeck climbed the rock in 1848 by the Old West Route, he left his name on the summit in a ginger beer bottle. Over the years many of the early pioneers who climbed the rock also left their names. But sadly, in June 1876, when two navvies scaled the rock the bottle had disappeared.

After completing the climb of Pillar Rock a short grade 1 scramble can be enjoyed to the summit of Pisagh. This is made from the col where the main path climbs towards Pillar mountain. The top of Pisagh gives very good views.

After all the scrambling continue to climb Pillar mountain, which provides a superb panorama and for many is one of the finest summits in Lakeland. From the summit of Pillar head south-west to Wind

Gap, where a rapid though rough descent can be made back to Wasdale Head if desired. Ideally, continue the walk over to Scoat Fell and Red Pike above the great combe of Mosedale. Descend the long and stony path to a col. Yewbarrow can then be climbed via Stirrup Crag followed by the long descent back to the shore of West Water.

*Pillar Rock from the south*

# WISTOW CRAGS

*A fine scramble on to Pillar, making an exciting alternative to the long walk up to Black Sail Pass from Wasdale.*

---

**Grade:** 3
**Quality:** ★★
**Distance:** 14km (8.5 miles)
**Total Ascent:** 1,190m (3,900ft)
**OS Map:** 89
**Time:** 5–6 hours
**Start/Finish:** Wasdale Head (GR 186097)
**Escape Routes:** The difficult sections are at the bottom and can be bypassed for easier alternatives.
**Notes:** There is a lot of loose rock particularly in the upper sections, and much of the rock is vegetated. Wait for a dry period. A rope, slings and selection of nuts should be carried.

---

The south-facing slopes of Pillar are often bypassed by walkers *en route* for Black Sail Pass before climbing Pillar. But closer inspection reveals a superb two-tiered rock buttress that leads from near the bottom of Mosedale to the summit of Pillar in a scrambling adventure of nearly 300m.

Follow the track from Wasdale Head into Mosedale. Leave the main path where it divides and follow the faint track towards Wind Gap.

As height is gained the obvious two-tiered buttress can be recognised above a fan of scree to the right of Wind Gap. It is the only major ridge in the area with a scree gully on the left and a narrow gill on the right.

Leave the track and head for the base of the crag. The scrambling begins at a grass terrace at its base on the left. The best scrambling follows a line up the left side throughout, often overlooking the precipitous scree gully. The main difficulties are at the start. The lowest broken rocks lead up the edge of the scree gully to a steep rock wall. Either bypass the difficulty by entering the gully on the left or walk to the right to scramble over a ridge.

The angle of the buttress then eases and a fine rib overlooking the scree gully can be climbed. The scrambling continues easily to a grass terrace. Ahead lies the second tier, but a blank slab makes progress difficult. Once again a ridge on the left overlooking the gully provides the key. Scramble up this to reach another terrace. Again walk to the left to pick a line up a rocky ridge overlooking the gully.

The scrambling eases and a short walk leads over a grass neck in the buttress. There are superb views here back down into Mosedale and it's worth taking a few moments to enjoy the solitude.

Once more the best of the scrambling continues on the left. The rocks are loose ahead and demand careful handling. A series of short ridges made up of loose flakes build to a final flurry of good scrambling. All that remains is a short walk over boulders to the summit of Pillar.

There are plenty of opportunities to continue the day's walk. The best option is to complete the Mosedale Horseshoe by heading south-west to Wind Gap, Scoat Fell, Red Pike and Yewbarrow. For more scrambling, head north off the summit down the narrow rib that links Pillar mountain to Pillar Rock. You can then tackle the Slab and Notch (Route 5).

*Scrambling on Wistow Crags, Pillar*

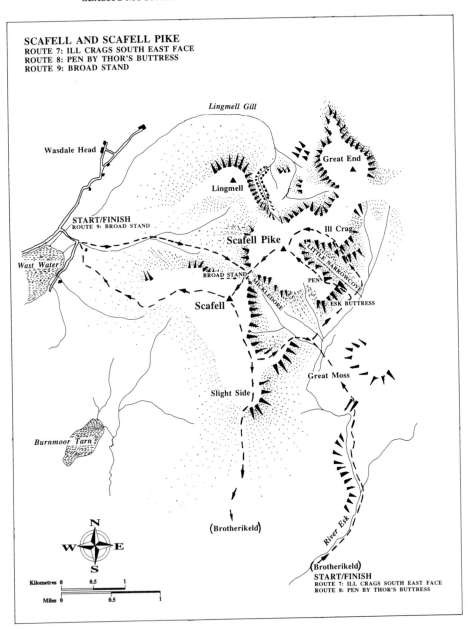

**SCAFELL AND SCAFELL PIKE**
ROUTE 7: ILL CRAGS SOUTH EAST FACE
ROUTE 8: PEN BY THOR'S BUTTRESS
ROUTE 9: BROAD STAND

42

# INTRODUCTION TO THE
# SCAFELL RANGE

Scafell Pike, England's highest mountain, and Scafell lie at the heart of the Lake District. Around these summits there are superb cliffs and stunning mountain scenes that are comparable with any other in Britain. The range contains a number of summits all above the 900m contour. At the north-eastern extreme is Great End. Its north face regularly provides excellent winter climbing, but the rock is too fragile for any scrambling or climbing sport.

The most southerly summit of the range is Scafell, from where long slopes lead down to Eskdale via Slight Side. Some more adventurous walkers use this route as an approach even though it is long. To the east of the range is the hidden wilderness of Upper Eskdale which is too far from any roads to ever become crowded – a lengthy walk in from either Eskdale or Langdale are the only routes of approach. But here there are cliffs and wild mountain scenery that can only be witnessed by those who like a good long walk or who are prepared to carry a tent.

At the foot of the range on the

*Scafell and Scafell Pike viewed across Wast Water*

43

west lies Wasdale Head. It is a long drive to Wasdale Head, even these days, but it was here that many of the early pioneers developed the sport of rock-climbing in England. On the north side of Scafell is a 180m-high rock wall. This is one of the greatest rock-climbing cliffs in England and has hosted many historic climbs.

The summit of Scafell Pike is only easily attainable from the west and even then it is a long haul. Its neighbour, Scafell, is even more difficult to climb. The linking ridge between Scafell and Scafell Pike is Mickledore, but it is necessary to complete the grade 3 scramble of Broad Stand to cross between the two peaks directly. Many walkers take a route via Foxes Tarn to avoid this problem. The other popular route between Scafell and Scafell Pike follows Lord's Rake across the north face of Scafell, and this is often regarded as the walker's route.

There are a number of well-trodden paths in the range but it is fairly easy to get off the beaten track and discover a whole new world of adventure. The eastern side of the mountain holds some of the best scrambles in the Lake District. Long, broad, rocky ridges rise from Upper Eskdale to the summits of these most popular mountains, often without another walker being in sight until you reach the top.

# ILL CRAGS

*A 400m scramble over a broken mountainside on the quieter side of Scafell. This makes for an excellent approach to England's highest mountain.*

---

**Grade:** 3
**Quality:** ★★★
**Distance:** 18km (11 miles)
**Total Ascent:** 1,100m (3,600ft)
**OS Map:** 89 or 90
**Time:** 6–8 hours
**Start/Finish:** Brotherilkeld Farm, Eskdale (GR 212012)
**Escape Routes:** There are breaks between the difficult sections but once a section has been started it is very difficult to escape except by down-climbing the route.
**Notes:** A rope and selection of nuts and slings are recommended throughout particularly as route-finding can be difficult.

---

Upper Eskdale is quiet with only backpackers, climbers and dedicated day walkers venturing forth. Remember that the remoteness adds serious overtones to an accident when help will be many hours' walk away.

The long walk in from Eskdale is wonderful in itself. Park at the bottom of Hardknott Pass near a telephone box and walk down the lane towards Brotherilkeld Farm. A sign points the way past the farm along the bank of the River Esk. The walk to the waterfalls of the Esk is popular, so don't be too surprised to meet a few day-trippers *en route*.

Having taken in the views of Esk Falls, the route becomes quieter as you enter the remote combe of Great Moss in Upper Eskdale. The skyline panorama of mountains must be one of the finest in England. The Scafell massif dominates the view and forms a superb backdrop to Great Moss, a soggy sponge from where the waterfalls of the Esk sap their water.

It is worth climbing on to High Gait Crags to take in the view and identify the line of the scramble. Scafell is on the left, with the deep notch of Mickledore leading across the skyline to Scafell Pike. Esk Buttress is the huge rock wall in front of Scafell Pike, and Little Narrowcove is the long scree gully further to the right. The small rocky summit just to the right of Esk Buttress and to the left of Little Narrowcove is Pen. There is a classic scramble to this summit by Thor's Buttress (Route 8). To the right of Little Narrowcove is Ill Crags. There is a long broken line of crags leading up the north-east side of Little Narrowcove to its summit, and this is where our route leads.

There are two prominent areas of continuous rock, with a more broken sloping slab between. This route

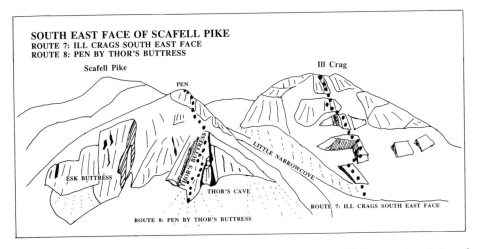

tackles these three sections of good rock to reach the summit of Ill Crags.

Approach the bottom of the scramble by negotiating the broken outcrops just to the right of Little Narrowcove. Head for the steep wall, with an impressive block above and clean rocks to the right. There are endless route possibilities in these early stages.

Once below the steep wall climb the clean buttress to the right of the vertical wall by the nose to reach a heather terrace. Escape by a groove on the right then follow a rake to a mossy slab. Follow a line up slabs to a grass terrace below a section of slabs. The slabs look very difficult but there is an easy route up them. On the left there is a heather groove. The route traverses from the right back left to gain a ridge above this groove.

A short wall at the top leads to easier ground with a scree run on the left. Walk across the scree to the base of a steep clean wall. To the left is a V-gully which provides a very difficult approach to the easier rocks above. Alternatively, climb the broken ridge of flakes to the right of the wall.

Easier ground leads to a steep buttress on the left. Once again easier rock can be climbed on the right to avoid the difficult buttress. To climb the buttress a rope is advised. Climb the edge until it steepens. Then move left as things start getting serious. Gain a groove then step back right. Climb up on good holds for about 6m then move left to gain the left edge of a rib before popping over the top to easier ground.

A final flurry of relatively easy scrambling continues up a broken ridge. The difficulties ease and quite suddenly you arrive on the summit of Ill Crags. Just like the trade routes to Scafell Pike, Ill Crags provides a superb viewpoint. To continue the walk head for Scafell Pike over the boulder-strewn summit plateau.

To end the day either drop down Mickledore and walk back out from Upper Eskdale or crack Scafell while you're in the area. The scrambler's route is Broad Stand (Route 9). Alternatively, walk to Scafell via the Foxes Tarn path.

From Scafell the best descent is the long steady route over Slight Side, though this will leave you with a short road walk back up Eskdale to Brotherilkeld Farm. Alternatively, return to Upper Eskdale via the ridge over Cam Spout Crag.

*Scrambling on the long central slab section of Ill Crags south-east face, Upper Eskdale*

# PEN BY THOR'S BUTTRESS

*An ideal route to Scafell Pike's satellite summit of Pen, far from the crowds and with a superb approach from Eskdale.*

*Grade:* **3**
*Quality:* **★★★**
*Distance:* **16.5km (10.5 miles)**
*Total Ascent:* **1,020m (3,340ft)**
*OS Map:* **89 or 90**
*Time:* **6–8 hours**
*Start/Finish:* **Brotherilkeld Farm, Eskdale (GR 212012)**
*Escape Routes:* **Only by retracing the route of ascent.**
*Notes:* **There is some wear on this route but route-finding skill is still required. A rope, slings and selection of nuts are required.**

The summit rocks of Pen are rarely visited, though there is excellent rock all around. The scrambler can take advantage of this and enjoy a truly memorable day exploring the crags.

The best approach is from Eskdale. Follow the route from Brotherilkeld Farm as for the Ill Crags route (Route 7). Once you arrive at Upper Eskdale pick out the huge rock-face of Esk Buttress overlooking the Great Moss, with scree at its foot. To the right of Esk Buttress there is a scree gully and then another slab buttress. There is a distinct vertical black crack split-ting the crag; this is Thor's Cave. Above the crack the summit of Pen can be seen. To the left of Thor's Cave is a long, gently sloping slab which extends to a lower level than the crack and divides the scree. This is Thor's Buttress and is the route taken by this scramble.

Clamber over the scree to gain the mossy lowest rocks on the but-tress. Gain a terrace to the left of Thor's Cave and below a corner crack. To the left of the crack there are some obvious large flakes. Walk to the left then follow a sloping shelf back right to a grass gully below the flakes. Climb up the gully to the top flake. Traverse left by squeezing between the flake and the crag. Continue to the left over a long bilberry terrace to its end. Climb a short rock step, using a juniper root as a hand-hold, to gain the top of a square block.

Easier rock walls lead back to the right to overlook the gully. On the left is a series of smooth slabs with an obvious huge perched boulder lying on the slabs. Follow these back left across the buttress. Join a bilberry terrace at the end of the slabs and continue to traverse along this until the rock on the right eases its angle. At a mossy scoop climb up and traverse right to overlook the gully once more.

There is an unstable-looking perched block. Walk to the left along the base of a steep wall. After about 7m there is a rocky groove

*Upper Eskdale en route for the Great Moss. Scafell Pike can be seen directly ahead*

that can be climbed to easier ground above. The buttress then eases and a final walk and scramble lead to the summit rocks of Pen. This vantage-point affords superb views, and it's worth taking time to savour them.

If a short round is required then it is possible to descend into Little Narrowcove. But care and good visibility are required for there are plenty of steep crags.

To continue the walk to Scafell Pike, scramble easily up the remaining two rock tiers. A short walk leads to the summit of England's highest mountain.

End the day with a scramble up Broad Stand (Route 9) to Scafell. Alternatively, follow the path via Foxes Tarn. A descent can then be made either by a long steady walk down Slight Side to Eskdale or by a short scrambly walk down Cam Spout Ridge to the Great Moss via Cam Spout Falls. This is the best round and leaves you with a long but easy walk out along the banks of the River Esk.

# BROAD STAND

*Probably the most famous difficult step in the Lake District. Broad Stand provides a direct link between Scafell Pike and Scafell.*

---

**Grade:** 3
**Quality:** ★
**Distance:** 8km (5 miles)
**Total Ascent:** 870m (2,850ft)
**OS Map:** 89 or 90
**Time:** 4–5 hours
**Start/Finish:** Wasdale campsite (GR 182075)
**Escape Routes:** Only escape is to retrace scramble.
**Notes:** This route often catches walkers out. Don't attempt it solo unless very experienced. A polished route that is best avoided when wet. A rope, slings and selection of nuts are recommended.

---

The most direct link between Scafell Pike and Scafell is via Broad Stand. The difficulties only last for around 2.5m, but this short step has made many turn back and forced others to call for help from passing walkers.

In many ways the route is too short to be a classic but its fame has blown its quality out of proportion.

It was probably one of the first climbs to have been made in the Lake District. On 5 August 1802, the poet Samuel Taylor Coleridge clambered down from Scafell to Mickledore by what is now known as Broad Stand. Today, climbers often use it as a way of descent, but even some of them have trouble with it.

From Wasdale walk to Mickledore on the main path via Hollow Stones. Broad Stand starts a few feet down on the Eskdale side of Mickledore at a narrow cleft in the rock-face. Squeeze through this and follow the well-polished route around the left and up to the sloping platform below a steep corner. This is the most difficult move. It is only around 7.5m above Mickledore and 2.5m high, but it is slightly overhanging and a slip will send you tumbling all the way back to Mickledore. The holds on the corner are often wet and greasy. Dry conditions along with a degree of agility and strength are required, while a rope is very comforting.

After the difficult corner the route eases into simple scrambling and walking to the top of Scafell Crags. The summit of Scafell is then close. Descend to Wasdale via the path over long slopes leading west from the summit of Scafell.

*Scafell viewed across Mickledore from Scafell Pike*

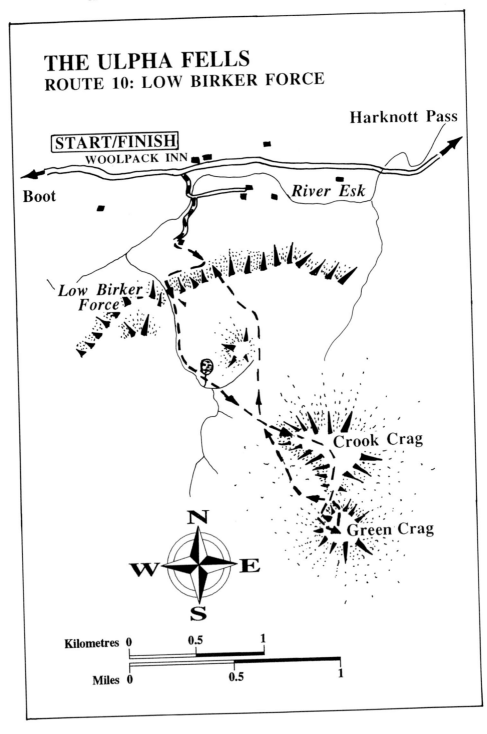

# THE ULPHA FELLS
## ROUTE 10: LOW BIRKER FORCE

Harknott Pass

START/FINISH
WOOLPACK INN

Boot

River Esk

Low Birker Force

Crook Crag

Green Crag

N
W E
S

Kilometres 0     0.5     1

Miles 0     0.5     1

# INTRODUCTION TO THE ULPHA FELLS

If you have made the pilgrimage over the road from Dunnerdale to Eskdale you would have crossed the Ulpha Fells. They cover the vast area to the west of the Coniston Fells and to the south of the Scafell group. But you probably had your eyes set on the mightier peaks to the north, so may only have given them a passing glance.

The most famous summit in the area is Harter Fell. It is a superb satellite peak that provides a clear viewpoint when the rest of Lakeland is veiled under a cloak of cloud. To the west of this lies a huge expanse of rolling moorland with crags jutting out from every corner. Two of these sprouting crags are Great Whinscale and Green Crag, the latter at 489m being the highest in the area after Harter Fell. They form a jagged backbone along the crest of the Ulpha Fells and are the centre of attention for this chapter. Green Crag lies on the fringe of fellwalking in the Lake District. To the south and west the scenery has little to offer, so any exploration of these hills begins to their north in Eskdale.

Eskdale is a superb valley that is largely bypassed by most walkers. It is a long drive round or a day's walk away from the popular walking centres of Langdale or Borrowdale. When the central fells are in cloud a good day of walking can still be enjoyed in Eskdale. Harter Fell is easily climbed and there is plenty of low-level walking available.

For the scrambler Eskdale is an excellent base. On sunny days you could drive round to Wasdale or walk to Scafell Pike. To approach Scafell Pike along the River Esk into Upper Eskdale is, for me, one of the finest walks in the country.

For a low-level scramble the Esk Gorge is a superb day out – though with a soaking assured, it is best to return back down the valley without continuing to the tops. If the clouds should roll in then scramblers can turn their attention to the Ulpha Fells.

There is a worthwhile route on Harter Fell via its north-west crags. But perhaps the finest mountain route in the area follows Low Birker Force and then continues with more scrambling to Great Whinscale and Green Crag.

# LOW BIRKER FORCE

*An expedition into one of Lakeland's quieter corners. The gill scramble culminates in a fell walk and scramble on to the summits of Crook Crag and Green Crag.*

---

**Grade: 3**
**Quality: ★★**
**Distance: 10km (6 miles)**
**Total Ascent: 520m (1,700ft)**
**OS Map: 96**
**Time: 6–7 hours**
**Start/Finish: At the entrance to a lane leading to Penny Hill Farm, Eskdale (GR 189009)**
**Escape Routes: The gill can be left at a number of places for the left bank.**
**Notes: Best to wait for a dry spell. A rope, slings and selection of nuts are recommended.**

---

As you drive along Eskdale from Boot towards Hardknott Pass, Low Birker Force can be seen on the south side of the valley, just past the Woolpack Inn. When in flood, it produces a white flash on the fellside, with a huge head waterfall cascading over the rim of the Ulpha Fells. The gill flows through a narrow ravine with a canopy of trees in its lower stretches. This route scrambles up Low Birker Force then continues on to the boggy plateau of the Ulpha Fells.

Begin the day by parking along the Eskdale road where a small lane leads towards Penny Hill Farm. There is only space for a couple of cars on the side of the road. Walk down the lane towards the farm and follow the bank of the River Esk. Cross the river on Doctor Bridge then immediately turn right down a lane signposted to Low Birker. The lane climbs above the level of the River Esk to pass the buildings at Low Birker. At a path junction after the buildings, turn sharp left to climb above the buildings. The path leads around the east of a plantation to a wall with a gate at the top.

Walk through the gate and follow the stone wall all the way to the

*Low Birker Force in flood, Eskdale*

bottom of Low Birker Force. Small cascades spring from beneath the trees and the route seems to disappear into the depths of the wooded ravine.

The scrambling begins easily by tracing the bed of the gill. Soon a cascade blocks easy progress. Climb a rib on the left and continue scrambling until the main falls come into view. The headwall appears impossible to overcome, but you can climb it from the left on a series of slabs in a steep corner. Soon the angle eases and a steep ridge leads to a tree. A short move to the right leads to a ledge, then a steeper section to another tree.

Finally, a traverse to the right leads to the base of the main cascade. It is impossible to climb this waterfall directly. Escape left to a grass ramp leading up the edge of the cascade. A footpath continues over the falls and the top of the scramble is reached.

If a short day is required follow the path down the side of the gill to Low Birker. For a longer day, head for the boggy delights of the Ulpha Fells where more scrambling beckons.

Follow the stream-bed to Low Birker Tarn and head for the lowest crags of Great Whinscale. These produce around 100m of scrambling and lead to the summit of Crook Crag. The scrambling is exposed, at an easy angle and at a lower grade than Low Birker Force. There are plenty of opportunities to make this final section as easy or as difficult as you wish.

The scramble begins at the lowest rocks, to the right of a prominent pinnacle that can be seen on the skyline. The route then swings from left to right picking out the best sport. From the top of Crook Crag the neighbouring summit of Green Crag is only a few strides away. If you are still keen then you could have a final scramble here.

The scrambling is reached by descending west from Crook Crag. Walk around the base of the steep crags to clean, easy-angled rocks. Climb up these rocks then swing right to pick up a line over more outcrops. A final section of slabs further to the right leads up the south-western side of Green Crag. At a height of 490m this is the highest point on these crags. It is a superb viewpoint with the Lakeland fells lining up to be counted and recognised.

To end the day follow the path along the west side of the crags which leads back to Low Birker and Penny Hill Farm in Eskdale.

# INTRODUCTION TO THE BUTTERMERE FELLS

The twin lakes of Buttermere and Crummock Water are enclosed by the Buttermere Fells. To the north of the lakes stand Grasmoor, Robinson and Dale Head. They are formed from Skiddaw Slate to produce smooth, rounded, grassy fells which provide delightful fell-walking country.

To the south of the valley the High Stile Ridge forms the long mountain barrier as far as Hay Stacks, with Fleetwith Pike plugging the southern end of the valley.

These fells are predominantly carved from volcanic rock with rough crags and steep rock-faces.

Of all the fells in the Lake District, the late Alfred Wainwright requested that his ashes be scattered on Hay Stacks. This clearly speaks for the area's outstanding beauty. Scenically, the range is stunning, with constantly changing views in all directions. Within their general contours are areas of rolling grassy hills, rough crags, tumbling waterfalls and intricate gorges.

*The view across Buttermere to Robinson from Burtness Combe*

To most observers Grasmoor is a great domed mountain with steep scree and grass slopes. But closer inspection reveals the long line of Lorton Gully, splitting the south-western slopes above the scree line. This provides an entertaining scramble from the roadside to the summit of the mountain. The High Stile Ridge has high hanging valleys carved into its northern face. These contain much loose rock and are slow-drying, but in good conditions are home to many classic rock-climbs. Between the steep rocks in Burtness Combe there is a section of crags known as Grey Crags that can be linked into a wonderful open scramble. The route leads directly to the summit of High Stile part way along the main ridge.

One of the historical classic lines in the range is Sourmilk Gill which issues from Bleaberry Tarn below Red Pike. But this gill has been the scene of a major landslide, leaving the rocks liable to tumble into the valley at any time. There have been many accidents here, so this very dangerous route cannot be recommended.

At the head of the Buttermere valley lies Fleetwith Pike, with its long nose dipping towards Buttermere. The north face of this mountain is steep and slow-drying, but given good conditions provides a steep scramble from Honister Pass to the summit of Fleetwith Pike. The scrambler is then ideally placed to head for a short round of Hay Stacks or a longer walk to Great Gable.

# LORTON GULLY

*A scrambling adventure with a pioneering air about it that leads on to Grasmoor.*

---

**Grade:** 3
**Quality:** ★★★
**Distance:** 8.5km (5 miles)
**Total Ascent:** 870m (2,860ft)
**OS Map:** 89
**Time:** 5–6 hours
**Start/Finish:** Lanthwaite Green (GR 159207)
**Escape Routes:** It is possible to exit the gully at many places, but there is no escape while scrambling the hard pitches.
**Notes:** Best climbed during a dry spell. The rock is lichenous and proves very slippery when wet. If there is too much water in the gill many sections become impossible. A rope, slings and nuts are recommended.

---

Grasmoor doesn't attract the same amount of visitors as some of the other fells in Buttermere. But if you really want to escape the crowds head for Lorton Gully on its western flanks.

There is parking space along the road in Lanthwaite Green. From the carpark beside Lanthwaite Green Farm the long winding line of Lorton Gully is clearly visible, rising above the scree to the summit of Grasmoor.

To avoid a head-on ascent of the scree, find the path with a finger-post pointing towards Grasmoor just outside Lanthwaite Green Farm. Follow this over soft grass to climb the north-west shoulder of Grasmoor. As height is gained good views open up all around.

Once the north-west ridge is reached, traverse right across the top edge of the scree. Walk around the base of a number of crags then cross a final scree run to reach the scoop at the base of the gully.

The gully begins with a series of water-washed blocky steps. A trench-like gully is then entered.

*A staircase of rocky steps in Lorton Gully, Grasmoor*

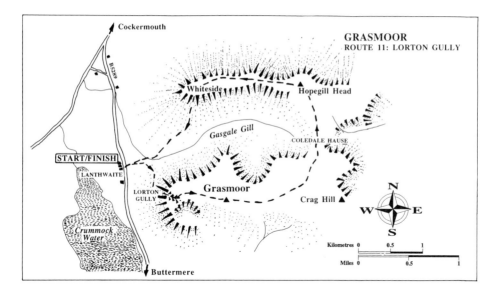

The route is easy at first and the short rocky difficulties are soon negotiated. Heather and juniper sprout from every crevice and come in useful as handholds. The feet need to jam into cracks for the best holds.

At a bilberry bay a narrow section lies ahead. There are steep walls of rock on both sides and a jammed boulder at half height. A square chimney leads to a short but steep scamper out of the difficulties. All these sections are avoidable on the right, but if you're having trouble now it would be better to retreat before the real difficulties begin.

A short chimney is best climbed by bridging to reach an alcove with a slab and steep wall beneath an overhanging holly tree. From above the slabs, escape right through a cleft in the rock to reach another bilberry terrace. Ahead there is another steep and narrow gully which enters a dark chasm. This is the crux of the route. A boulder practically blocks the entrance. Squeeze past this and follow the stream into the chasm. Ahead, a series of falls lead forever upwards. This next section is inescapable once started, so move cautiously.

The holds are hard to find in places but with perseverance the first steep step is conquered. A 5m chimney proves slightly easier and can be climbed by bridging. A ledge is reached for a brief rest. The hardest section is a steep and mossy 7m wall which leads to a comforting ledge.

Ahead the route enters an open amphitheatre. Avoid the red rock on the right and take a route about 30m to the left that enters an open V-shaped gully. Easy steps lead through the gully to a final jammed boulder that provides the final difficult step to break out of the gully.

After some easy terrain, the gully splits. Take the left branch until it loses its interest. The best line is then to continue on the left over the North-West Ridge of Grasmoor.

59

The flat, grass-covered summit of Grasmoor has a huge cairn to shelter behind while the wind whistles over the plateau. The route for the remainder of the walk is now within our sights. Follow the well-worn path to the east to reach Coledale Hause. Climb up the long southern slope of Hopegill Head via the thigh-burning scree slopes of Sand Hill.

Finally, follow the broad ridge west to Whiteside. A long descent drops down over Whin Ben and crosses Liza Beck to end the expedition.

# GREY CRAGS

*A superb high-level scramble set in a remote combe carved into the north side of the High Stile Ridge.*

---

**Grade:** 3S
**Quality:** ★★★
**Distance:** 14.5km (9 miles)
**Total Ascent:** 400m (1,300ft)
**OS Map:** 89
**Time:** 6–7 hours
**Start/Finish:** Gatesgarth (GR 194149)
**Escape Routes:** It is possible to escape from the route between the main scrambling sections.
**Notes:** A rope, sling and selection of nuts are required. The route links a series of crags by their easiest line, between various difficult rock-climbs. Rock-climbing experience is desirable and the route should be climbed roped-up throughout for safety. Wait for a long period of sunny dry weather before attempting this route.

---

The traverse of the High Stile Ridge is one of the grandest prizes for the Lakeland walker. The ridge gives superb views in all directions and once gained provides easy walking. But to score this goal requires a lengthy slog up one of the paths at its ends. Neither of these is very pleasurable. For those with a background of high-level scram-bling or rock-climbing there is a far more interesting alternative.

The series of combes scooped out of the northern slopes of the High Stile Ridge provide a stunning panorama. They are often cloaked in cloud and as they face north require a long, dry spell before they become safe for climbing. Given good conditions they provide the finest route to the High Stile Ridge. This route tackles Grey Crags in Burtness Combe, below the summit of High Stile.

*Combe Beck issuing from Burtness Combe, Buttermere*

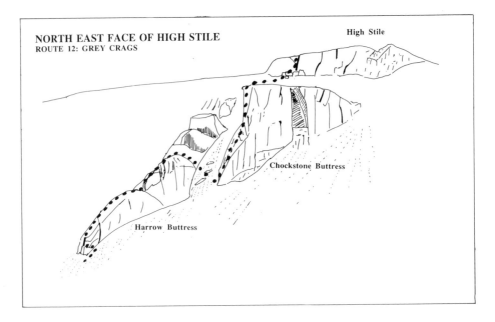

NORTH EAST FACE OF HIGH STILE
ROUTE 12: GREY CRAGS

High Stile

Chockstone Buttress

Harrow Buttress

Begin the day at Gatesgarth at the head of Buttermere, where parking is available. Follow the path for Scarth Gap along with those walkers bound for Hay Stacks. Where the main path swings left for Scarth Gap, leave it and continue climbing towards Burtness Combe. The track climbs steadily below Low Crag to a plaque dedicated to two mountain rescue team members who died while practising their abseiling skills in 1969.

The track is faint but eventually leads to the stream issuing from Burtness Combe and a stile over a stone wall. Climb the stile and walk into the heart of the combe.

Ahead one of the biggest crags in Lakeland hangs dark and foreboding from the head of the combe. To the right are the smaller series of crags known as Grey Crags, lying above a fan of scree. Climb along a vague path towards the scree, then begin the short struggle to the base of the crags.

The lowest crag is Harrow Buttress. Above this is Chockstone Buttress. There are scree chutes up both sides. The crags provide a number of popular low-grade rock-climbs so scramblers should have a rope in case they drift on to climbing rather than scrambling terrain.

The scramble begins by tackling Harrow Buttress. A direct ascent would be possible but is given a grade of Difficult in the climbing guides. Instead, traverse in from the right on a ledge to gain a narrow, deep chimney up the centre of the buttress. Climb this for 7m then escape left. Climb up towards an overhang then escape left once more. Easier scrambling leads to the top of this first buttress, where stunning views across the hanging valley to Dale Head and Fleetwith Pike can be savoured.

Climb up easier broken rock to a gully on the right. Further to the right is the obvious pillar of Chockstone Ridge. This is the next section of the scramble. Walk down into the gully to reach the base of the buttress.

The scramble up Chockstone Ridge is 72m long and graded as Moderate in the climbing guides. Some climbing experience and a rope are required. Climb the ridge on a series of steps to the right of a gully and left of a crack. Near the top there is a difficult tower. Step around to the left into the gully to escape if necessary. From behind the tower move right then left to regain the crest of the ridge and follow it to a ledge. More difficulties appear ahead. The route takes the chimney on the right but this

has a difficult exit. If preferred, escape left into the gully and climb to the right to pass a chockstone.

A grassy platform leads to a final rock buttress. There are plenty of opportunities to find a way over these and this final scramble leads to the summit of High Stile.

To return to where you started the day, walk east to Scarth Gap. If a rapid retreat is required then head directly back down the pass to Gatesgarth. For a better round continue over Hay Stacks, soaking up the views to Gable, Kirk Fell and Pillar *en route*. The day ends with a round of Fleetwith Pike, where there are exceptional views down Buttermere and along the entire High Stile Ridge. A long steep walk down the western nose of Fleetwith Pike leads to Gatesgarth.

*Scrambling over the top of Harrow Buttress on Grey Crags, Buttermere.*
*Fleetwith Pike is in the distance*

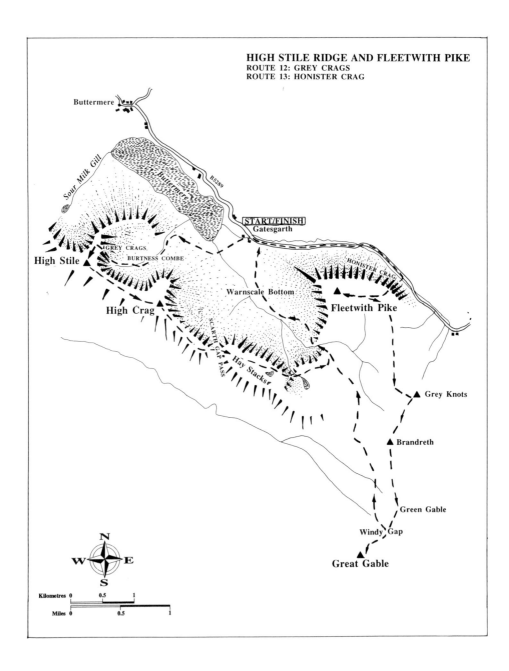

HIGH STILE RIDGE AND FLEETWITH PIKE
ROUTE 12: GREY CRAGS
ROUTE 13: HONISTER CRAG

# HONISTER CRAG

*On the north side of Fleetwith Pike the 300m high Honister Crag overlooks the pass. The rock is loose in places but this rock wall provides challenging open-face scrambling.*

**Grade:** 3S
**Quality:** ★★
**Distance:** 16km (10 miles)
**Total Ascent:** 1,050m (3,460ft)
**OS Map:** 89 or 90
**Time:** 6–7 hours
**Start/Finish:** Gatesgarth (GR 194150)
**Escape Routes:** There is no easy escape once the route has been started.
**Notes:** The rock is loose in places, so a helmet should be worn. Avoid the route in the wet. Good route-finding ability is essential. A rope, slings and selection of nuts are recommended. The route should be climbed roped-up throughout.

Anyone who has driven over the Honister Pass cannot fail to be moved by the towering rock wall of Honister Crag. At its base there is scree and large tumble-down boulders, looking ready to roll a little further down the pass in a gust of wind. Above this there are rocky gullies and outcrops that blend into the main wall. The rock is littered with grass terraces and dark seepage stains. The crag faces north, making it a particularly dark and inhospitable place at any time other than high summer.

Begin the day at Gatesgarth on the Buttermere side of Honister Pass, where parking is available for a small fee. Walk up the road towards the top of the pass. Just before reaching the last bridge stop at a lay-by. From this point there are two main buttresses separated by a gully. The scramble follows a line up the left-hand buttress.

*The exposed flake on Honister Crag, Fleetwith Pike*

The climb starts with a frustrating two-steps-up-one-step-down clamber over the scree. There are some large boulders that can be followed to ease the pain slightly.

The scrambling begins with an easy assault of a slabby buttress. Steep and loose rock soon makes progress less secure. This is a good introduction to the route, for it sets the standard that is to follow. Grass terraces criss-cross the crag at this stage and it would be easy to bypass the difficulties, but beware of being led into a false sense of security.

After the slab a slanting scree terrace is crossed and a rock wall climbed to gain a curved scree chute. Walk right and follow a zig-zag line through the buttress. At the edge of a large slanting terrace beside the Central Gully, climb sheep tracks to overcome a heathery buttress to a small rowan tree.

Climb a steep earthy gully to a small amphitheatre with a large dark recess at its rear. The difficult scrambling now begins. On the left of the alcove is a short rock-face (which is desperate if wet) leading to a terrace with a rowan tree. The terrace overlooks the gully on the right and now the scrambler is totally committed.

A rope is recommended for protection and holds should be checked carefully. Climb directly up steep vegetation, then traverse left to a difficult rock step. Descend slightly to a ledge, then move up to some gun-like perched blocks. Arrange a belay here. Fortunately, there are some superb views to the pass far below and the distant northern fells, though the perch is rather too airy to linger long.

The grass terrace ends not far to the left where it overlooks a gully. There is no easy escape and the scramble seems foiled. But step back 2m to find the Achilles heel. Two heather-topped steps provide an escape and lead to a rib above. All is not yet over. Step left and make an exposed traverse of a large flake. Clasp your hands over the top while your feet make the most of the limited holds. Below your boots fresh air extends to the road in the Honister Pass. Arrive safely at a slanting rake just a couple of steps away from the exposed flake.

The difficulties ease and the slanting rake leads across the face to a tree. Clamber up the left of the tree to gain the old quarry railway line and mining tunnel that extends into the mountain. The rock is unstable, so resist the temptation to investigate further. Instead, follow the railway incline to its end then pick up a path through bilberry bushes to the top of the crag.

The summit of Fleetwith Pike lies to the west and can be reached by a path along the top of the crag. This is an ideal spot to take a break and let your pulse-rate recover from the exhilaration of the scramble, while you enjoy the views down the Buttermere valley.

To continue the day, head for Grey Knotts and Brandreth. Green Gable and Great Gable are then well within your stride. A descent can be made by heading west from Windy Gap. At a path junction turn right then follow the clear path over the western flank of Brandreth and down into Wanscale Bottom. A short walk leads to the start of the day at Gatesgarth.

*Napes Needle on the Climber's Traverse, Great Gable*

*The Sphinx Rock overlooking Wast Water on the Climber's Traverse, Great Gable*

*Scafell and Scafell Pike viewed across Wast Water*

*Scrambling on the south-east face of Ill Crags, Upper Eskdale*

*Sunset from Scafell Pike*

*Scrambling in Lorton Gully, Grasmoor*

*Buttermere from Fleetwith Pike*

*Walking into Burtness Combe below High Stile, Buttermere*

*Honister Pass and mine workings from Honister Crag*

*Above the clouds on Sharp Edge, Blencathra*

*Descending the chimney from the Attic Cave, Doves Nest Crags, Glaramara*

*Steep scrambling on Pinnacle Ridge, St Sunday Crag*

# INTRODUCTION TO THE
# NORTHERN FELLS

The great whale-backs of Skiddaw and Blencathra overlook Keswick, the capital of Lakeland. The mountains are best viewed from either Castle Crag across Derwentwater or from Castlerigg Stone Circle. From both they dominate the skyline. At 931m Skiddaw is Lakeland's fourth highest mountain and Blencathra at 868m is the fourteenth highest.

The two are divided by a deep cleft where Glenderaterra Beck flows. To the north of these summits is the vast wilderness known simply as "back o' Skidda'". Dash Beck flows north-west and the River Caldew flows north-east to divide this wilderness. To the north of these river valleys lie the lower Uldale and Caldbeck Fells. They look more like an area of Bleaklow or the Pennines than the Lake District. It comes as no surprise that these are some of the quietest areas in Lakeland. Walkers rarely wander this way except to visit Skiddaw House, one of the most isolated youth hostels in the country, or perhaps to walk along the Cumbria Way *en route* for Carlisle. The smooth, grass-covered slopes of the North-

ern Fells have few crags on them. Skiddaw is one of the most popular fells for walking in the Lake District and hundreds of tourists climb it each day. But few climbers or mountaineers would exchange a day on the crags of Scafell for a day on Skiddaw. The terrain is all very easy and the main paths well worn.

Blencathra, though, has more to offer the adventurous walker. From the north it appears to be no different to Skiddaw or "back o' Skidda'", but from the south it can be seen that there is much more to this mountain. Travelling north over Dunmail Raise, it is hard to overlook the ridges that sweep down from the long summit ridge to the valley near Threlkeld. The ridges of Gategill Fell, Hall's Fell, Doddick Fell and Scales Fell all provide good ascents to Blencathra. Between these ridges the routes of Blease Gill, Gate Gill, Doddick Gill and Scaley Gill provide adventure for scramblers, but none of these can compare to the superb Sharp Edge. This is by far the mountain's finest route and is the scramble described in Route 14.

# SHARP EDGE

*If you've conquered the walker's ridge Striding Edge and want to progress on to something more difficult, head for Sharp Edge. For many it is their first real scramble.*

---

**Grade:** 1
**Quality:** ★★★
**Distance:** 11km (7 miles)
**Total Ascent:** 660m (2,160ft)
**OS Map:** 90
**Time:** 5–6 hours
**Start/Finish:** Scales (GR 340269)
**Escape Routes:** Some of the difficulties can be bypassed by following a path below the north side of the crest. The route can be retraced in case of difficulties.
**Notes:** One of the most popular of the easier scrambles. Go early or late in the day to avoid the crowds.

---

Sharp Edge is a well-established classic. It was the scene of one of the first rock-climbing photographs taken by the legendary Abraham brothers of Keswick in 1890. The photograph shows the two young brothers breaking all the rules of modern rope craft and was later captioned by George Abraham "How not to climb".

For the scrambler Sharp Edge is the finest approach to the summit of Blencathra, in the northern fells of the Lake District. This grade 1 route is equivalent in difficulty to the traverse of Crib Goch in Snowdonia, but Sharp Edge is far shorter.

For the optimum excitement stick to the crest. In high winds, or if the rock is icy, a path can be used that traces a line below the crest on the north side. Boots have polished the holds over the years so that today there is no difficulty in following the classic route.

The day begins in Scales along

*High on Sharp Edge with snow on the ground*

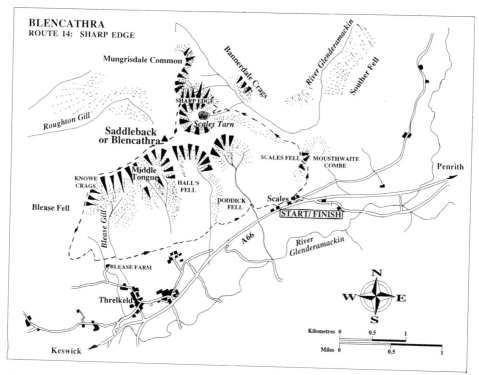

BLENCATHRA
ROUTE 14: SHARP EDGE

the main A66 highway from Keswick to Penrith. A lay-by provides ample parking space even for busy weekends. Climb steadily from the roadside up through farm buildings and around the eastern flank of Blencathra. The path is clear and leads gradually around the base of Scales Fell. Height is quickly gained and there are extensive views over the Lakeland fringe to Great Mell Fell, a prominent conical landmark standing alone in a patchwork of fields.

Traverse the left bank of the River Glenderamackin on a raised grass terrace. Scales Beck is eventually crossed and the path followed to Scales Tarn. The tarn is set in a combe with the headwall leading steeply to the summit of Blencathra. The jagged skyline to the north is Sharp Edge. Don't be tempted to

take a dip in the still waters of Scales Tarn. It rarely sees the sun and has been described as the coldest tarn in Lakeland.

The path is clear as it climbs from the peaceful shoreline of Scales Tarn to the jagged crest of Sharp Edge. Look for polished holds and follow the crest as it begins its airy passage to the tops. The experienced and the purist will find scrambling along the crest a delight, being high, exposed and sharp. There are tremendous views both ahead and behind.

If things are becoming too risky then head for the safer path below the north side of the crest. But whichever route you take at first, you meet a narrow slash in the ridge providing a testing challenge; there is no easy way. A steady head, a deep breath and a couple of confident strides take you over the worst, possibly with a feeling of relief if this is your first ridge scramble.

The ridge now starts to lose its identity as it joins the main Blencathra massif. A long steady scramble up easy slabs is all that remains. In the wet these can be treacherous and it is best to stick to a worn path that swings to the left. In dry weather it is possible to make a direct assault to the top.

The summit plateau of Blencathra is a bare expanse of grass. A clear path swings around the rim to the summit cairn at 868m.

To continue the walk it is best to make the long traverse of the summit plateau west towards Skiddaw. This is a gently undulating walk with extensive views to the central fells. At the end of the whale-back, follow the path that sweeps around to the south into the valley bottom. Follow the line of a stone wall back east along the base of Blencathra to return to the start of the day at Scales.

If you want a shorter round then descend directly from the summit of Blencathra down Hall's Fell Ridge.

# INTRODUCTION TO GLARAMARA

At the head of Borrowdale the three satellite valleys of Stonethwaite, Langstrath and Seathwaite enclose Glaramara. The fell is separated from the Scafell Range by Esk Hause. Though of minor significance to its neighbours Scafell and Great Gable in terms of grandeur, Glaramara is highly regarded among scramblers. On this one fell are four classic lines including a buttress, ridge, gill and even a cave scramble.

Borrowdale as a whole is littered with crags. Climbers have been discovering new test-pieces since the Abraham brothers started putting up routes in the 1890s. For scrambling purposes many of the crags are too short to produce classic mountain lines, though for shorter days on the hills there is a lifetime's worth of adventure.

Many of the scrambling lines were first discovered by Bentley Beetham with the Goldsborough Club of Barnard Castle School. The routes were often graded as Moderate or Difficult rock-climbs and many still are today.

Glaramara is divided into a horseshoe by Combe Gill. This enticing, glaciated hanging valley is one of Lakeland's finest scrambling areas. Here you will find the long, slender Intake Ridge that knits together a series of crags near the mouth of the combe.

Further on towards the head of the combe is a clean buttress on the left. This is Doves Nest Crags. The route here climbs into a cave part way up the crag, known as the Attic Cave, then escapes to climb around the outside to gain the tops. The cave was formed by a huge rock-slide. There are warnings posted on the fell gate stating that it is dangerous to explore the caves of Doves Nest Crags. This refers to the cave system behind the main face, not the route described here. However, the rock may move again at any time, so climb here at your own risk. You have been warned.

Two more routes exist around the outside of Glaramara. One is Cam Crag Ridge, which climbs from the secluded dale of Langstrath in spectacular fashion to the west of the Glaramara summit. This route has the added bonus that it can be made as difficult or as easy as you like.

Finally, the scramble up Grains Gill and over Allen Crags complete the varied exploration of Glaramara. This route tops out to the south of the Glaramara summit and is ideally placed for a climb to Scafell Pike.

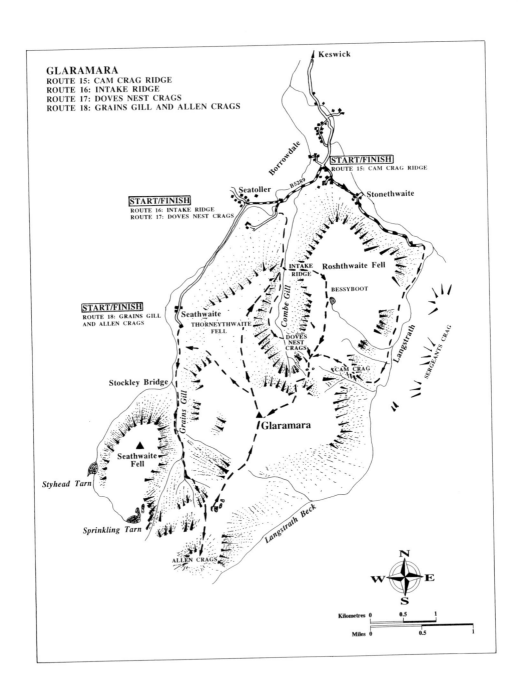

GLARAMARA
ROUTE 15: CAM CRAG RIDGE
ROUTE 16: INTAKE RIDGE
ROUTE 17: DOVES NEST CRAGS
ROUTE 18: GRAINS GILL AND ALLEN CRAGS

Keswick

Borrowdale

START/FINISH
ROUTE 15: CAM CRAG RIDGE

B5289

Seatoller

Stonethwaite

START/FINISH
ROUTE 16: INTAKE RIDGE
ROUTE 17: DOVES NEST CRAGS

INTAKE RIDGE

Roshthwaite Fell

BESSYBOOT

START/FINISH
ROUTE 18: GRAINS GILL AND ALLEN CRAGS

Seathwaite

THORNEYTHWAITE FELL

Combe Gill

DOVES NEST CRAGS

Langstrath

SERGEANT'S CRAG

CAM CRAG

Stockley Bridge

Grains Gill

Glaramara

Seathwaite Fell

Styhead Tarn

Sprinkling Tarn

Langstrath Beck

ALLEN CRAGS

N
W E
S

Kilometres 0    0.5    1
Miles 0    0.5    1

# CAM CRAG RIDGE

*The broad buttress of Cam Crag Ridge provides around 220m of almost perfect scrambling terrain. It lies at the end of a quiet valley, the rock is sound and the route can be varied to suit your ability.*

---

**Grade: 2**
**Quality: ★★★**
**Distance: 10.5km (6.5 miles)**
**Total Ascent: 680m (2,230ft)**
**OS Map: 89 or 90**
**Time: 4–5 hours**
**Start/Finish: Stonethwaite (GR 262137)**
**Escape Routes: Easy options on the left of the route allow difficulties to be bypassed. The route can be used as a descent.**
**Notes: There are no route-finding problems. The rock is sound with good holds. A rope is recommended.**

---

Cam Crag Ridge was discovered by Bentley Beetham with the Goldsborough Club of Barnard Castle School in 1943, and is graded as Moderate in the climbing guides. Since that time it has become a popular classic.

Start the walk from Stonethwaite. Walk up the valley along the south-western bank of Stonethwaite Beck. The surroundings are quiet and the walk relaxing. The path leads through a campsite on its journey towards Eagle Crag.

The rock buttress of Eagle Crag overlooks the gateway to Langstrath. On it climbers test their skill and nerves on routes such as Where Eagles Dare and Dead On Arrival. Turn south below Eagle Crag to enter Langstrath. The path follows the line of the Cumbria Way, a 113km trans-Lakeland walk from Ulverston in the south to Carlisle in the north.

Follow Langstrath Beck up the valley, pass White Crag on the right and about three-quarters of a kilometre further is Cam Crag Ridge.

*The start of the scramble over Cam Crag Ridge, Glaramara*

73

Its jagged outline first appears arcing over the flanks of Rosthwaite Fell. From this angle the route looks quite imposing. From the base of the crag the rock stands proud like a stepped backbone curving over the fellside. The rock looks clean and the line to the tops is clear.

The ridge is gained by traversing a disordered array of boulders. Start the scrambling at a steep rock wall. Climb the wall on the left and then continue over a sharp rib. The broad buttress of the ridge is now ahead. The scrambling is wonderful, with good juggy holds appearing just as they are required. A variety of routes is possible, but for the best grade 2 scrambling stay on the right. At any difficulties it is always possible to step left on grass

terraces to avoid getting into trouble.

Follow a series of diagonal cracks up each rock wall. The first crack steepens into a corner, but good holds allow an escape. The steep sections are split by grass terraces which provide excellent viewpoints, particularly to the High Raise massif behind. The short scrambling sections gradually become easier as height is gained. But there is a sting in the tail: care is required on the last wall where the holds are less well frequented and some loose rock exists.

The scramble ends on the rough and marshy terrain of Rosthwaite Fell. Walk over to Glaramara from where it is possible to follow the tourist path down Thorneythwaite Fell to Borrowdale.

*The head of Langstrath from the end of Cam Crag Ridge, Glaramara*

# INTAKE RIDGE

*One of Bentley Beetham's classic discoveries. Intake Ridge is a ridge scramble that is broken into short testpieces. When combined with a walk over Glaramara, it provides a classic round.*

**Grade:** 3
**Quality:** ★★★
**Distance:** 10km (6 miles)
**Total Ascent:** 680m (2,230ft)
**OS Map:** 89 or 90
**Time:** 6–7 hours
**Start/Finish:** Carpark at Seatoller (GR 246138)
**Escape Routes:** The route is broken into short sections of scrambling. It is possible to join or leave the route between any of these sections.
**Notes:** The rock is secure and well worn. There are some route-finding difficulties. A rope and selection of nuts and slings are recommended.

Bentley Beetham discovered Intake Ridge in 1937. He was a bold innovator of rock-climbs who took part in early Everest expeditions. He graded the route Moderate. Since then it has become a Borrowdale classic. If difficulties become too great then an escape is easy. These days the route is given a scrambling grade of 3.

The ideal circuit to be combined with an ascent of Intake Ridge is to climb to the summit of Glaramara, a hill often visited, though most walkers will use the tourist route which clings to the slopes of Thorneythwaite Fell. Intake Ridge is set on the eastern slopes of Combe Gill below Rosthwaite Fell. The valley is littered with craglets and is a paradise for the scrambler.

From the carpark at Seatoller, walk east to Mountain View cottage. A path opposite, signposted Thorneythwaite, leads towards Combe Gill. Climb a stile on the left which crosses a field to climb up

*Scrambling on Intake Ridge, Glaramara*

through a coppice of holly and rowan, with sheep quietly grazing. Follow a stone wall around the foot of Thorneythwaite Fell. The crazed outline of Intake Ridge is now visible ahead on the left. Continue along the path to a kissing gate where the stone wall ends. Pass through this then descend to the water's edge and ford the beck.

Intake Ridge is now directly above. The start of the route is reached by climbing up steep, rough scree alongside the stone wall. Where the wall ends the first outcrop of the ridge eagerly awaits your presence on the right. There is around 200m of scrambling ahead. It is broken into short, sometimes tricky, sections.

The route begins with a cleft up the left of a huge flake at the base of the outcrop. Good jugs make light work of the difficulties and a small platform is soon gained. Easy-angled rocks lead to a grass verge. Walk right for about 7m to another rock rib which is longer and more continuous than the first. Step across to a grass platform at the base of the steep rock barrier. Step left once more and climb the clear face of rock on good bucket-holds for the hands and small pockets for the feet for about 3m. The holds are perfectly spaced, providing wonderful flowing scrambling. Easy-angled slabs continue towards the skyline. At a steepening in the slabs escape left to reach a safe platform from where broken rocks lead to the base of an imposing rock wall.

Escape to the right on some narrow slabs and step carefully

*Scrambling on Intake Ridge, Glaramara*

around a corner to a huge, flat scoop in the rock. It is a vertical drop over the edge, so don't get too close. The scrambling now becomes a little tricky and a rope may be required.

Ahead lies a dome of rock which is vertical at your feet before gently curving over on to easier terrain. The sides drop down steeply and it looks like a formidable obstacle.

There are two options, of which the first is slightly easier. A ramp on the right looks easy but don't get too optimistic. The crux isn't reached until you're committed near the top. Easy moves lead on to the slab and then an awkward bulge has to be negotiated. This is best achieved by careful footwork with a high step up left before rocking over on to the narrow platform above. Thankfully, an easy rising traverse then winds around to the top without difficulty but with tremendous exposure and what can only be described as "a lot of down".

The harder alternative begins at a crack on the left of the face. The crack is steep and slants to the right before joining the previous approach. Both routes up this slab are difficult to protect with a rope, so good scrambling ability is required.

At the top of the glaciated slab there are classic views down the combe to Skiddaw, Derwentwater and Honister Pass. Eroded paths on the left and right may make you wonder if many people bother with the scrambling section just conquered.

A narrow grassy walk continues to the next scrambling section. From here on the route is less distinct, but this is the best line I could follow.

A path crosses some scree to the base of a broken rib. Climb a moss and heather groove, 5m to the right of the base of the steep rock on the left. Wear marks clearly show the line of attack and easy scrambling brings you to the end of the groove. The escape is over mossy rock on the left, with good holds leading up to the crest above. A grassy broken ridge continues to another steep section. Step around the right on a grass terrace to find a platform at the edge of a gully. Climb directly up a steep wall to the left of a nose of rock. Good holds lead to a ledge. Walk around the slabs on the right to find easy ground with the open fells ahead. A short steep climb leads on to Bessyboot, where a number of cairns lead to a small tarn.

To complete the round follow a track that winds a dizzy line across Rosthwaite Fell over countless false summits and outcrops. The summit of Glaramara has two cairned tops to choose from, so it's best to visit them both to be sure of truly bagging the peak.

The first well-worn path of the day descends steeply from Glaramara back down the slopes of Thorneythwaite Fell to Combe Gill and the start of the day in Borrowdale.

# DOVES NEST CRAGS

*A once-popular playground over a series of landslipped boulders. The rocks are still liable to move so the traditional route into the Attic Cave via the Rat Hole is bypassed for a safer scrambling expedition.*

*Scrambling through the 'cave' of Doves Nest Crags, Glaramara*

**Grade:** 3
**Quality:** ★★
**Distance:** 9.5km (6 miles)
**Total Ascent:** 680m (2,240ft)
**OS Map:** 90
**Time:** 5–6 hours
**Start/Finish:** Seatoller (GR 245136)
**Escape Routes:** Some tricky moves on the route are difficult to escape from without rope protection. It is necessary to down climb the route from the cave.
**Notes:** There has been a notice on the fell gate since 1979 warning that due to recent rock-falls it is dangerous to explore the caves of Doves Nest. This refers to the caves behind the huge rock-face which used to be reached via the Rat Hole. The route described here avoids these areas, but the rocks are still liable to further movement. A rope, slings and selection of nuts are recommended.

Doves Nest Crags in the upland valley of Combe Gill are unlike any-thing else in the Lake District. They were formed when a giant slab slipped down the fellside to rest against the rocks below. There are cavities and crevices behind.

Andrew Thomson of Kendal and Millican Dalton of Essex, along with other climbers from Kendal, discovered that potholing could be combined with climbing on Doves Nest Crags. Until the late 1970s it was a popular expedition for adven-turous school groups to worm their way through the caves via the Rat Hole. You could keep dry on a scrambling route through the cave, but you weren't completely out of the wet because water would seep down the walls and drip from the roof.

A rock-fall in the summer of 1979 brought an end to that era, though. A sign was posted on the fell gate warning of the dangers of venturing too far and it is thought that the rocks are still liable to further movement. You have been warned.

The crags are approached by walking up Combe Gill as if heading for Intake Ridge (Route 16) from Seatoller. Continue up the west bank of Combe Gill until the main path swings up towards the ridge that leads to Glaramara. Leave the main path here and follow a faint track that continues along the bank of the gill to the head of the combe. Stay above the boggy depths until you see the square, clean buttress of Doves Nest Crags on the left. Walk around the head of the combe then climb steep scree on the right of the crags.

The path leads to the foot of the main crags. On the left there is a huge gap where the rock has split away from the main crag. Go around the front of this to a chimney on the far left. Climb into the depths of this chimney and squirm under a chockstone through a strenuous 3m channel. A scratched arrow on the right points to the historic Rat Hole. But heed the warnings and don't follow that route. Instead, traverse the balcony to the left and step into a V-groove that leads to the cave. Climb this with difficulty, then step right. The expedition should end by crawling through a hole above to the Attic Cave, but due to the dangers it is best to stop here as the boulders look very loose. The view is superb and it's a great perch from which to consider the descent.

The descent back down the V-groove is actually easier than the ascent. From the foot of the crags the exploration can be continued with a scramble up the sides. Return to the right of the crags by retracing the route of ascent. Scramble easily up a corner to a ledge. Continue up the corner on good holds to reach a flake on the right. Climb this then move right. Climb up easily for 5m then move back left to a rock platform.

Climb up again towards a rowan tree then move left up a groove and around a detached block. Move left along a narrowing block and make an exposed move up to reach the top of the main crags.

Slabs continue over the fells to reach the tops. Glaramara is now only a short walk away. A long steady descent down the main path over Thorneythwaite Fell ends the round.

# GRAINS GILL AND ALLEN CRAGS

*This scramble investigates the deep and wet ravines of Grains Gill, then opens out on to airy buttress scrambling over Allen Crags. Glaramara is then only a short walk away.*

---

**Grade:** 2
**Quality:** ★★★
**Distance:** 9km (5.5 miles)
**Total Ascent:** 650m (2,130ft)
**OS Map:** 89 or 90
**Time:** 5–6 hours
**Start/Finish:** Seathwaite, Borrowdale (GR 235123)
**Escape Routes:** There are many opportunities to escape from Grains Gill and Allen Crags throughout the route.
**Notes:** The gill would be impassable after a long period of rain and is best enjoyed in a dry spell.

---

The wettest place in England is Seathwaite at the head of Borrowdale, which means you might as well do some gill scrambling while you're in the area because it's bound to be raining.

This route follows the tourist path towards Sty Head as far as Stockley Bridge. The line of Grains Gill is then clearly in view ahead leading to the distinctive V-shape ravines on the hillside where the gill divides into its tributaries. From here the scramble leaves the con-fines of the gill for the airy buttress scramble over Allen Crags.

From Stockley Bridge follow the path up the west bank of Grains Gill. Shortly after where the stone wall ends enter the gill on easy boulders. Gradually the ravine narrows and the gill becomes engulfed in the canopy of overhanging trees. A series of small pools are reached adding extra interest. Easy routes are always possible on either the left or the right.

At the entrance of Ruddy Gill a waterfall cascades gently over the right bank. A pool at its base is circumnavigated on the left and then the watercourse is followed up a narrow ravine. When the ravine narrows further, the options decrease. Fortunately, good handholds are available to prevent a slip. A rising ramp on the left is followed. It is wet and slippery but not technically difficult. It provides superb scrambling with wonderful rock scenery and plant life all around for the botanist scrambler. The right wall hangs over the gill at an ominously steep angle. This looks particularly unnerving because of the large cracks that bear witness to how fragile the rock is in places. As befits the wettest area in England, the ravine walls trickle with water continually. A wet sleeve and neck is the unavoidable outcome of the route.

There is a large jammed boulder that blocks the ravine. A wet ascent up the left side overcomes the obstacle and allows entry to the remainder of the gill.

If you have had enough it is possible to make an escape up the left bank to the open fellside above the ravine. Easier scrambling over jammed boulders continues to a large cave – a mining scar from the past.

The watercourse swings to the left and small cascades roll over thin quartz veins in the rock. The ascent on the left of this is slippery, so to avoid an accident take the grass on the right bank. A series of small cascades continue up the gill.

The scrambling reduces to a walk as the ravine opens out and the watercourse is followed on to the open fell to two prominent trees. The scrambling begins once more where the river bends to the left.

Low-grade scrambling leads over short cascades into the jaws of the ravine at the base of the V-shape seen from the start of the route. The scrambling increases in difficulty as the waterfalls grow in size. At some of the more difficult falls direct wet ascents are possible, although an escape from the wet can be made on the left or right. A short, steep wall with waterfalls tumbling over the left is more demanding and requires a difficult climb on its right or a complete bypass via a route further to the right. The ravine narrows from now on and the scrambling becomes more difficult.

After two small falls an escape path is taken on the left wall to safer terrain above. The route then follows the left bank of the ravine, passing two grass bays. At the second of these cross the ravine to a

*Scrambling on Allen Crags, Glaramara*

*Grains Gill, Glaramara*

rock buttress on the right bank; this is Allen Crags.

Walk over to a rib and take the heather groove up its left. Walk back right to the crest of the rib. A high reach is useful here to gain the small grass terrace. There is loose rock in places and you quickly find yourself in some dramatic situations. This is all difficult and by far the hardest section of the route so far. The rocky rib is very exposed. Fortunately, there is an easier grass route on the left that bypasses the action.

A short but steep corner provides the next challenge and leads to a steep wall. Walk around to the right. Follow a path which leads to a ramp and a vertical break in the rock. A tough scramble up this gains the top of the ridge once more. If this is too difficult then walk around the grass further to the right to join the route higher up. Suddenly the panorama opens out, so take a break to admire the views to Great Gable, Glaramara and Skiddaw.

Ahead lies the impressive barrier of another rock prow. Walk to the left where a line can be taken up a grassy, rough and rocky gully. A bilberry terrace is traversed back right in an exposed position with a particularly airy step to gain the rock rib above the prow.

The scrambling eases now and the high fells are well within your sights. Glaramara is easily reached and provides the natural continuation of this scramble. A descent past Hind Gill leads back to Seathwaite.

# INTRODUCTION TO THE HELVELLYN AND FAIRFIELD RANGE

Helvellyn is one of the most popular summits in Lakeland. For many years before surveying became a science, Helvellyn was regarded as the highest summit in the region. For many people it is their first (and often only) Lakeland summit. Over the years the summit has seen motorcycles, mountain bikes and, in 1926, an aeroplane.

Helvellyn lies halfway along the longest mountain range in the Lake District. To the west the range presents an uninteresting smooth face over Dunmail Raise. To the east the ice has bitten deeply into the mountains, leaving fine buttresses and wild hanging valleys. To the north of Helvellyn are the grassy, rounded summits of the Dodds with Clough Head marking the most northerly point of the ridge. These hills are quiet and rarely visited by all but the enthusiastic Wainwright-bagger. To the south of Helvellyn the ridge has a number of tops with Dollywagon Pike marking the end of the main ridge, overlooking Grisedale Tarn. Bounding the southern side of the

*Dollywaggon Pike and Helvellyn from Deepdale Hause*

Grisedale valley is the fine whale-backed fell of St Sunday Crag, often regarded as the connoisseur's mountain of Lakeland.

Fairfield is the southerly extension of the Helvellyn ridge and, once again, it has some fine wild valleys with steep crags on its eastern side. The most famous feature of the Helvellyn and Fairfield range is Striding Edge. The ridge begins near Glenridding on the east of Helvellyn and builds to an airy climax. It is the most popular scrambly walk in the Lake District – and probably in Britain. Wainright's Coast to Coast path traverses the ridge and on busy weekends there are queues along its crest. To the north of Striding Edge lies Swirrel Edge. This ridge is usually included in a round of Striding Edge and Helvellyn from Glenridding. But neither of these two ridges can be classified as scrambles. The diffi-cult sections are short-lived and easily bypassed.

To find good scrambling in this range it is necessary to search for routes in the uninspiring western slopes. These are mostly found among the Dodds to the north of Helvellyn, where there are some superb deep ravines. These are the basis for a number of classic gill scrambles in the following pages. There is also the fine broad buttress of Brown Cove Crags on the northern side of the Helvellyn summit, with a wonderful gill leading directly to its foot.

The finest ridge in the range is Pinnacle Ridge on St Sunday Crag. A classic line along a jumble of pinnacles, it has long been popular with adventurous souls. Finally, on the eastern side of Fairfield, there is one of Lakeland's finest gill scrambles tucked away at the head of the peaceful valley of Deepdale.

# SANDBED GILL

*An inescapable adventure into the depths of a deep ravine in St John's in the Vale. At the end of the scramble the springy turf of the Dodds provides a walk of great contrast.*

---

**Grade:** 3S
**Quality:** ★★★
**Distance:** 13.5km (8.5 miles)
**Total Ascent:** 740m (2,430ft)
**OS Map:** 90
**Time:** 6–7 hours
**Start/Finish:** Carpark in St John's in the Vale (GR 318196)
**Escape Routes:** The route is only escapable by retracing your steps. At the beginning it is possible to bypass the route by following a path up the left bank.
**Notes:** The rock is often slippery and the route is best climbed during a dry spell. A rope, slings and a selection of nuts should be carried for the crux of the route. Waterproofs are advisable.

---

The eastern wall of St John's in the Vale comprises steep mountain slopes that lead to the Dodd fells. There are places in the slopes where mountain streams have carved deep gullies between the crags. One of these streams is Sandbed Gill, beginning on the fell tops in a boggy hollow, below Clough Head. On its journey it has created a deep ravine where it disappears from view until finally spouting from beneath trees in the valley bottom. This ravine is where some of Lakeland's finest gill-scrambling sport can be found.

Start the expedition from the carpark beneath Castle Rock at the entrance to St John's in the Vale. Sandbed Gill is the most northern of the gills along the valley. The start of the scramble is located just to the south of the road leading into Bram Crag Quarries. Follow the road through the quarry and cross a stile leading on to the fellside. The gill is then directly on the left, its entrance guarded by trees.

Enter the narrow ravine at a large tree. The route is obvious – you simply follow the gill. The rock is loose in places and some vegetation on the holds can be troublesome, especially in the wet. The difficulties in the scramble involve steep climbs over wet rocky walls.

The scramble is easy at first. Soon the watercourse narrows and the handholds and footholds lose their size. The right wall overhangs the gill bottom and water droplets peel away from long strands of rich green vegetation. Flowers cling to soggy cracks in the rock and creatures scamper for cover as the stream beats a line between boulders.

The steep, slimy bed of the gill makes progress hazardous. A series of steps up the left wall are the easier

*Scrambling in Sandbed Gill, St John's in the Vale*

The crux of the route comes at a forbidding rock ramp leading up the left side of a waterfall. The slab is the only way up and gives a sustained climbing pitch of about 10m. Some laybacking technique is required; work hand over hand up a rising crack while your feet search for holds. This section will require a rope by all except the very confident. Good belays are available above the problem.

The scrambling eases now and the gill opens out into a fine amphitheatre of fell, fungi, water and rock. The gill can be followed to its demise in a soggy hollow on the tops. A final stroll over soft turf leads to the summit of Clough Head. There are tremendous views from this quiet fell top. Blencathra and Skiddaw hold centre stage to the north, while all around fell tops wait to be recognised and counted.

To complete the round of the Dodds, walk south over the gentle grass fells to Calfhow Pike, an oasis of rock in a green desert. Great Dodd, Watson's Dodd and Stybarrow Dodd all fall as easy prey to the peak-bagger and form a relaxing contrast to the earlier action of the day.

Descend down Sticks Pass to the roadside at St John's in the Vale.

option and these lead to a grass terrace. A precarious series of moves then lead delicately back to the gill itself.

Jammed chockstones in the bed of the gill form delightful waterfalls and swirling pools. Most of the boulders can be negotiated on the left or right but a soaking is assured during any ill-directed reconnaissance.

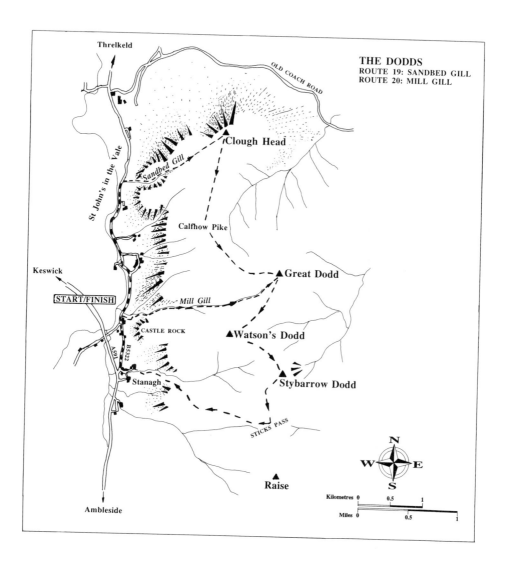

THE DODDS
ROUTE 19: SANDBED GILL
ROUTE 20: MILL GILL

Threlkeld

OLD COACH ROAD

Clough Head

Sandbed Gill

St John's in the Vale

Calfhow Pike

Keswick

START/FINISH

Great Dodd

Mill Gill

CASTLE ROCK

Watson's Dodd

B5322

Stybarrow Dodd

Stanagh

STICKS PASS

Ambleside

Raise

N
W    E
S

Kilometres 0     0.5     1
Miles 0          0.5     1

# MILL GILL

*This is one of Lakeland's long-standing classic gill scrambles. The route rises in a long succession of cascades for around 180m.*

---

**Grade:** 3S
**Quality:** ★★★
**Distance:** 9.5km (6 miles)
**Total Ascent:** 750m (2,470ft)
**OS Map:** 90
**Time:** 4–5 hours
**Start/Finish:** Carpark in St John's in the Vale (GR 318196)
**Escape Routes: The gill can be bypassed at various places but some moves are quite committing. A rope should be taken to aid retreat.**
**Notes: The route is only feasible during a dry spell. The rock is very wet and mossy even after dry weather. A rope, slings and selection of nuts are recommended.**

---

The route is easy to follow; you simply trace the line of the gill. Most of the falls can be negotiated except for one just after the start. A couple of pools are best waded through so choose a hot summer's day for the ascent.

The day begins at the carpark on the southern end of St John's in the Vale. Take the path east towards Castle Rock, a favourite climbers' haunt. This leads into the woods then follows a stone wall towards the base of the crag. At the top of the wall traverse left above the plantation to the edge of Mill Gill. The gill can be seen erupting from beneath overhanging trees in a series of waterfalls.

Begin by climbing the first waterfall on the right. If there is too much water then the pitch, and therefore the scramble, will be impossible. Having overcome the first fall you enter a chasm with a more difficult fall ahead.

This is bypassed on the right by back-tracking up the side of the ravine to the bank above the falls. Walk to the top of the falls then return easily back to the ravine. The next series of waterfalls are climbed on the right. Tree roots are used for handholds as you balance precariously above the swirling pools of water.

At the top of these cross over slippery rocks then follow the bed of the gill. Cross a deep pool on the left to reach a junction where the route continues to the left. Climb the rocks on the left as the gill enters a ravine. At another deep pool with steep walls on either side make a daring traverse of the left wall or wade through the water and bridge up the waterfall beyond.

Good scrambling continues past numerous falls as the ravine leads forever onwards. The scrambling eventually ends and the open fells beckon. Continue walking to break out on to the tops. Great Dodd is the highest summit of the range and is only a short walk away. Bag this summit then stroll back down over the smooth grass slopes to take in Watson's Dodd and Stybarrow Dodd. The walk ends with a descent from Sticks Pass down to the road at the southern end of St John's in the Vale.

*Scrambling in Mill Gill, St John's in the Vale*

# BROWN COVE CRAGS

*One of the quietest ways of reaching the summit of Helvellyn. Delightful, easy gill scrambling followed by superb open buttress scrambling.*

---

**Grade:** 3 (1 in Helvellyn Gill)
**Quality:** ★★
**Distance:** 10.5km (6.5 miles)
**Total Ascent:** 865m (2,840ft)
**OS Map:** 90
**Time:** 4–5 hours
**Start/Finish:** Carpark along Thirlmere (GR 315170)

**Escape Routes: The ascent of Helvellyn Gill has many escape routes throughout. Brown Cove Crags is more serious and the only easy way is to continue up. Notes: Route-finding is very difficult on Brown Cove Crags. A rope, slings and selection of nuts are recommended.**

---

Helvellyn, at 950m, is one of the most sought-after summits in the country and it can be difficult to avoid the crowds. But as always the

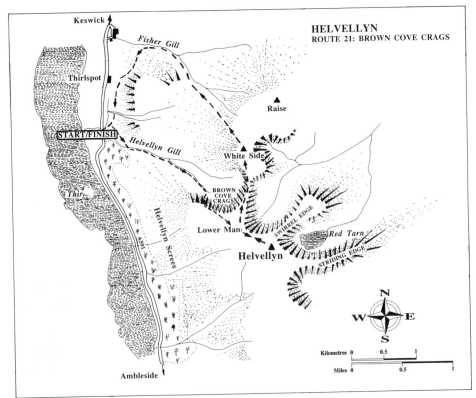

## HELVELLYN
### ROUTE 21: BROWN COVE CRAGS

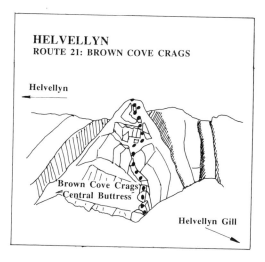

**HELVELLYN**
ROUTE 21: BROWN COVE CRAGS

Helvellyn

Brown Cove Crags
Central Buttress

Helvellyn Gill

scrambler can find the best routes, far from the crowds and full of adventure. This route gains Helvellyn via a scramble up Helvellyn Gill and Brown Cove Crags.

Park along the eastern shore of Thirlmere at the North West Water Authority carpark. Helvellyn's tourist route can be seen snaking its way up. To the left of this is the quiet ravine of Helvellyn Gill, its true nature hidden in its deep and winding course. Above this Brown Cove Crags projects from the main Helvellyn massif.

Follow the main path as far as a large wooden bridge that crosses the outflow of Helvellyn Gill. Wait for the walkers and tourists to disappear up the trade route and then duck into the ravine of Helvellyn Gill and follow its course to below Brown Cove Crags.

The scramble is grade 1 and is a fine approach to Brown Cove Crags. The rocks can be slippery and care is needed on every step. The quiet waters of Thirlmere gradually come into view along with the distant mountain skyline of the

Wasdale, Borrowdale and Buttermere fells.

Stay near the watercourse for the best sport and nip on to the paths up either side to avoid the difficulties. A large cascade spanning the ravine calls for some careful footwork up the left side over slippery rocks. The route criss-crosses the ravine as the water dances between swirling pools. Another large cascade is climbed on the left to reach a jammed boulder. Climb this on the left and risk a soaking, or on the right for a drier alternative. Gentle walking leads out of the head of the gill and into a soggy combe with Brown Cove Crags high on the right.

If you're not up to grade 3 scrambling then head across to the right and join the tourist path on to Helvellyn. If grade 3 scrambling is within your limits then the 150m stretch over Brown Cove Crags is waiting.

In the centre of the crags is the main buttress, which is longer than the others with a broad terraced base. On its right, a sweep of clean rocks rises to a narrowing rib which ends about 70m above the base, to the right of an obvious corner crack. The route climbs this rib then breaks through the steep wall via a small hole. Finding the start of the route isn't too difficult as there is a cairn that marks the spot. It is located about 20m up the right-hand side of the buttress, where a left-slanting gangway crosses the face.

Start along this gangway then move right to gain the rib. Follow this for around 50m. At a grassy gully and after countless false turns the rib ends. The grass rake provides an escape to the left but head right for more scrambling. The grass soon ends at a steep rock tower. Move to the right around some perched boulders, then climb a crack (not the short chimney with a jammed stone) on the left which leads to a corner at the side of the tower. To escape, crawl through a gap between wedged rocks known as Riley's Window. Above, twin grooves on the right of a large block lead to a grass rake. Walk for about 20m to a boulder then climb the ridges on the right that finally lead over to the summit plateau and the tourist path.

The summit of Helvellyn is a short walk away and stunning views abound. The descent can be taken by a number of routes including following the tourist path directly back down, but for a finer walk head for Lower Man down the ridge to White Side. To return to the car-park follow the path north-west over open grassy fells to Thirlspot. Stay above the walls and pick up a footpath that eventually leads back to Thirlmere.

# PINNACLE RIDGE

*The Lake District is not blessed with a multitude of ridge routes, though it does have one excellent example to make up for this deficiency. Pinnacle Ridge is one of Lakeland's finest scrambles.*

**Grade: 3**
**Quality: ★★★**
**Distance: 15km (10 miles)**
**Total Ascent: 950m (3,110ft)**
**OS Map: 90**
**Time: 6–7 hours**
**Start/Finish: Grisedale Bridge (GR 390161)**
**Escape Routes: All difficulties can be bypassed on the left or right of the main ridge.**
**Notes: A rope and selection of nuts and slings should be taken on this route.**

Pinnacle Ridge lies on the north face of St Sunday Crag, a peak somewhat over-shadowed by Helvellyn, one of Lakeland's most famous mountains. The ridge overlooks the hoards of tourists climbing up Striding Edge to Helvellyn. But that is where the similarity ends. Pinnacle Ridge is far more difficult and far less well trodden than its neighbour. The line is dramatic and invigorating. It is an enjoyable scramble with a developing interest that never exposes itself until the last minute. The scrambling is rarely desperate or over-committing. A path leads up the left side that could easily be gained if the going gets tough.

The route is aptly named, for it comprises a series of rock pinnacles projecting into the Lakeland sky. They can be seen from the base of the route and act as a prominent landmark. The ridge drops straight down to the gully on the right, hence the preferred scrambling is on the right, overlooking the gully.

Begin the day at Grisedale Bridge between Glenridding and Patterdale. Follow the track along Grisedale valley. After approximately 2km the Elmhow plantation is reached. Continue to the southwest end of the plantation from where a path zigzags up the fellside of St Sunday Crag. A further 20-minute walk brings you to a grass shelf. Contour south-west along the hillside where the path is followed to a scree-run at the base of Pinnacle Ridge. Ascend the side of the scree to the foot of the ridge where there is a cairn. Across the scree a wide gully appears on the left and our scrambling route leads up the ridge left of this. A prominent gun-like block projects from the ridge higher up, acting as another natural landmark.

After only a couple of moves the ridge begins to narrow, the gully on the right adding greatly to the exposure. At this stage it is easy to sneak over to the path on the left but try to stay on the gully side with the deep

93

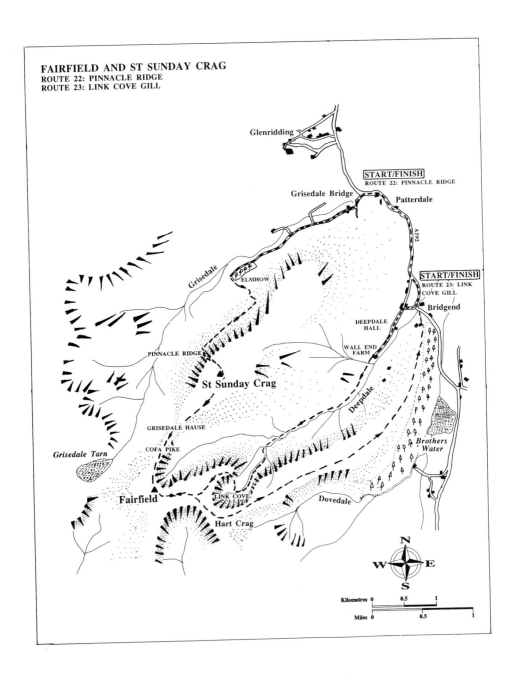

FAIRFIELD AND ST SUNDAY CRAG
ROUTE 22: PINNACLE RIDGE
ROUTE 23: LINK COVE GILL

precipice beneath your feet.

A giant cannon-shaped rock protruding from the ridge is soon reached. Its dark profile seems ready to fire a salvo over Grisedale. Climb on to its base and follow a narrow cleft to the right.

The route continues to unload giant pinnacles on the unsuspecting scrambler. The next confrontation is with a huge gendarme behind which a 6m rock wall blocks easy progress. This is the technical crux of Pinnacle Ridge. The key to the wall lies in its right corner where a wide crack rises to its top. The crack contains a chockstone that can be used as a belay. Once a start has been made up the corner crack the holds soon appear and the wall is conquered with surprisingly little difficulty. At the top there is ample opportunity for a leader to belay to protect a second.

A fine knife-edge of pinnacles stand guard before the final climb to the summit of St Sunday Crag. A steep drop on both sides hardly makes life any more comfortable, but it is the last problem to be overcome so breathe deeply and then carefully traverse the pinnacles, enjoying the airy situation on each delicate step. Immediately above, safe ground brings an opportunity to savour the position. What name would you give that route on its first ascent? What else could it be but Pinnacle Ridge?

The summit of St Sunday Crag is now a short walk away. It is a peak worth while in itself primarily for its views both to Helvellyn and across to the Fairfield ridge.

To continue the day descend to Deepdale Hause and climb Cofa Pike to the Fairfield summit. From here the whale-back of St Sunday Crag can be seen to its best effect. Walk over to Hart Crag and descend north-east over the long ridge of Hartsop above How to Deepdale Bridge. A short road walk returns you to Grisedale Bridge.

*St Sunday Crag from Fairfield*

# LINK COVE GILL

*A remote gill and crag scramble to the popular summit of Fairfield. This is one of Lakeland's most entertaining routes for the experienced scrambler and well worth the long walk in.*

**Grade:** 3
**Quality:** ★★★
**Distance:** 14.5km (9 miles)
**Total Ascent:** 721m (2,365ft)
**OS Map:** 90
**Time:** 5–6 hours
**Start/Finish:** Bridgend (GR 399144)

*Escape Routes:* **It is possible to escape from the gill and crag scramble at various places, but the rock can be slippery and a rope will be required.**
*Notes:* **Avoid after rain and in the wet. A rope, slings and selection of nuts will be required.**

Deepdale is a long valley flanked by St Sunday Crag to the north and Hartsop above How to the south. It provides a remote and exciting way

*Link Cove and Greenhow End seen from the approach walk along the banks of Deepdale Beck*

of reaching Fairfield at its head. Many walkers are put off by the 5km walk between the high fells, however, and prefer to follow one of the enclosing ridges. But for the scrambler the walk is a delight. It leads gently into the heart of the rugged and wild scenery that is hidden to all except those who are prepared to make the long pilgrimage.

The crags at the head of Deepdale were once a major centre for climbing until its neighbour, Dovedale, was discovered and the attention turned away. There is still much of interest here for the climber including some superb upper middle grade climbs on Hutaple Crag and Scrubby Crag.

This scramble follows the line of Link Cove Gill and continues over Greenhow End before finally arriving on the tops.

Begin from the Ullswater valley. There is limited parking at Bridgend beside a public telephone box along the A592. If this is full then park further down the valley at Patterdale or Glenridding and walk back along the road.

From Bridgend follow the track along the right of Deepdale Beck, signposted Deepdale. The track swings west to Lane Head, where it is necessary to turn left through a gate towards Deepdale Hall and Wall End. The track deteriorates as you head deeper into the dale. Eventually there is an obvious buttress of rock projecting from the head of the valley. This is Greenhow End. On its left is Link Cove and on its right Sleet Cove. Walkers follow the path into Sleet Cove to reach Fairfield, while scramblers

head for Link Cove. There are two streams issuing from the cove, the left one being Link Cove Gill and our target.

Where the valley path begins to rise above Deepdale Beck, leave it and pick up a fainter path across boggy ground towards Link Cove Gill. Cross streams and hummocky glacial moraines to reach the waterfall at the base of the gill.

The scrambling begins by climbing the open slabs to the left of the falls. The atmosphere then changes as the walls close in and the scramble enters the main gorge of the gill beneath a canopy of trees. The first problem arrives at a steep waterfall. Climb it on the right to reach another cascade. The rock is greasy

*Link Cove Gill in flood*

97

and care is required to climb and remain dry. Climb up on the right to gain a ridge above the ravine. A step down above the waterfall leads back into the gill. A deep pool is crossed to reach an amphitheatre of slabs with a waterfall. Climb left to escape. A rope is advisable here for the exposed top move. More waterfalls and slabs follow until the gill opens out into the hollow of Link Cove.

On the right is the obvious buttress of Greenhow End and this is our next objective. Many people walk up this by following a cairned zigzagging path, but more scrambling can be enjoyed by picking the best line over the rock to the left or right. Good friction makes the climb easier than that in the gill and height is quickly gained.

Fairfield is easily reached after the scramble. From the summit there are superb views along the Helvellyn range and over St Sunday Crag. This route descends back to Hart Crag and over Hartsop above How.

As an alternative round you might prefer to follow a descent from Fairfield over St Sunday Crag which would take you directly back to Patterdale in fine style.

*Fairfield from Great Rigg*

# INTRODUCTION TO THE LANGDALE FELLS

Many walkers have started their fell-walking apprenticeship on the Langdale Fells. On the road from Windermere to Ambleside the distinctive mountain skyline of the Langdale Pikes teases the eye, continually appearing and disappearing behind trees and buildings. The bold rock turrets of the Langdale Pikes are visible from many places in south Lakeland and from them all they are immediately recognisable.

The Langdale valley has much to offer, making it justifiably popular. There is a beautiful (though man-made) tarn, picturesque farm buildings and gently flowing rivers. High on the fells, the crags provide superb climbing sport and the lofty summits give exceptional views.

The Langdale Fells comprise the Langdale Pikes to the north of the valley, with Bow Fell and Crinkle Crags arcing around the head of the valley to Pike of Blisco on the south. The most popular summits are the Langdale Pikes, namely Pavey Ark, Harrison Stickle, Thorn Crag, Loft Crag and Pike of Stickle. These are often completed in one walk from the New Dungeon Ghyll Hotel at the base of Stickle Ghyll. The jagged skyline to the south of the Langdale valley is Crinkle Crags. This is also a popular round and many walkers link the traverse of Crinkle Crags with either Pike of Blisco to the east or Bow Fell to the north.

Throughout the valley there are gills to explore and buttresses to climb. For the scrambler there is an almost endless supply of sport. The bigger climbing crags such as Bow Fell Buttress and Gimmer Crag unfortunately do not provide anything within the realms of scrambling, though the smaller crags that litter the fellside provide plenty of opportunities. Many of them also face south, so they are fast drying.

The most popular scramble in the valley is undoubtedly Jack's Rake on Pavey Ark. For some walkers this is their first experience of scrambling. It is a classic diagonal line straight across the southern face of the mountain leading from the shore of Stickle Tarn to the summit of Pavey Ark. There are also a number of shorter scrambles on the remaining Langdale Pikes. On their own they are not as impressive as Jack's Rake, but when linked together they provide an excellent scrambler's round of the Pikes.

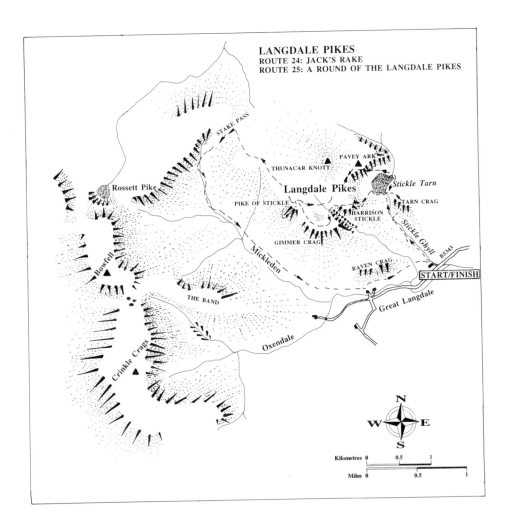

**LANGDALE PIKES**
ROUTE 24: JACK'S RAKE
ROUTE 25: A ROUND OF THE LANGDALE PIKES

# JACK'S RAKE

*One of the most famous scrambles in the country. Jack's Rake is the finest route to the summit of Pavey Ark.*

**Grade:** 1
**Quality:** ★★★
**Distance:** 14.5km (9 miles)
**Total Ascent:** 730m (2,410ft)
**OS Map:** 89 or 90
**Time:** 5–6 hours
**Start/Finish:** New Dungeon Ghyll Hotel carpark (GR 295064)
**Escape Routes:** Only by reversing the route, which is possibly more difficult than the actual ascent.
**Notes:** A very popular route best climbed early in the morning or late in the day.

*Looking up Jack's Rake, Pavey Ark, from the halfway point of the route, Langdale*

From the shore of Stickle Tarn, Pavey Ark shows its near-vertical south-facing cliffs. There is a full range of lines here for the climber – but is there anything for the scrambler? After a little close examination you will no doubt spot the diagonal weakness. A long narrow rake extends in a straight line from bottom right to top left. This is Jack's Rake and is probably the most famous scramble in the country.

Begin the day at the New Dungeon Ghyll Hotel. Follow the path up the banks of Stickle Ghyll which lead to Stickle Tarn. Alternatively, scramble directly up the beck. Walk to the right around the shore of Stickle Tarn and climb the scree to the base of the rake at the right-hand side of the crag. The scramble then begins up the long narrow cleft that climbs left across the cliff. Route-finding is simple – you follow the trough. There are rock climbs above and below the route so if you knock a block off, shout *"Below!"*.

*View over Stickle Tarn from top of Jack's Rake, Pavey Ark.*
*Windermere is in the distance*

You emerge from the confines of the groove about halfway up the climb, and suddenly there is a lot of down on the left. But the views are superb over Stickle Tarn and the Langdale valley.

From the open terrace a narrow groove is entered and the scramble continues to the end of the cliff-face. From the end of the groove a couple of rock steps prove to be the most difficult part of the climb. A clear path leads around to the left and up to a cairn by a stone wall. Walk back to the right to reach the summit of Pavey Ark.

The natural and most popular continuation of the walk is to com-plete the round of the Langdale Pikes. Walk over rough, rocky ground to Harrison Stickle, then drop from its delightful perch to the head of the Dungeon Ghyll ravine and take in Thorn Crag and Loft Crag. Follow a path along the edge of the fells above Gimmer Crag to the symmetrical cone of Pike of Stickle. Walk around the back of this to reach its summit by a short staircase of rocks.

Finally, descend to the valley by walking over boggy ground to Stake Pass. A long steady descent then leads down Mickleden to the New Dungeon Ghyll Hotel.

# A ROUND OF THE LANGDALE PIKES

*By combining the best scrambles in the area this route makes a complete traverse of the Langdale Pikes, one of Lakeland's finest group of summits.*

**Grade:** 1–3
**Quality:** ★★
**Distance:** 7km (4.5 miles)
**Total Ascent:** 760m (2,500ft)
**OS Map:** 89 or 90
**Time:** 5–6 hours
**Start/Finish:** New Dungeon Ghyll Hotel carpark (GR 295064)
**Escape Routes:** All of the scrambles can be bypassed, but once started the individual routes are difficult to escape from. A rope will be needed to safeguard an escape.
**Notes:** Best climbed during a dry spell. A rope, slings and selection of nuts should be carried.

The Langdale Pikes consist of Pavey Ark, Pike of Stickle and Harrison Stickle, while Thorn Crag and Loft Crag are the remaining lesser summits. This expedition links five scrambles around these summits.

The journey begins from the bottom of Stickle Ghyll. Enter the gill from the New Dungeon Ghyll Hotel carpark. Follow the path up the north side of the gill until the end of the fence is reached. It is now possible to begin the scramble through the bed of the gill.

The scramble up Stickle Ghyll is grade 1 but there are plenty of opportunities to make the sport more difficult. It is possible to escape from the gill on the left, but for the best action stick to the edge of the water. Soon a series of waterfalls build in grandeur to the final mighty cascade that provides a formidable barrier. This can either be bypassed or climbed from the right and crossed at mid-height.

The next objective, Tarn Crag, lies to the right and is clearly seen

*Scrambling on Tarn Crag, Langdale Pikes*

from above the fall. Leave the gill and scramble over scree to the base of the crag. Look for a large holly bush. Walk 6m past the holly to a ramp/groove rising to the left. There is a battered tree at half-height that helps identification, as well as a small rowan at the top.

The ramp gives a serious and delicate scramble at grade 3. There is a belay at the rowan. From the top of the ramp there are few problems and the hardest steps can be found on the right. Fine views abound from the summit of Tarn Crag over Stickle Tarn to Pavey Ark. To the left is Harrison Stickle, the focal point of the next scramble. By taking this route Jack's Rake on Pavey Ark can be left for the descent at the end of the day.

Walk down to the shore of Stickle Tarn and follow the path to the base of the east ridge of Harrison Stickle. The face is quite imposing on first sight, but with some care a line can be taken over the crags on the left. The rock is steep and, at grade 3, a confident scrambler is required for there is no way of making this section any easier. Above is a grass shelf with a second rock wall beyond. This wall is climbed direct and then a rising ramp from right to left is traversed. This provides exposed scrambling on good holds. To finish the route in style walk around to the south face of Harrison Stickle and climb a rock buttress to the summit at grade 3 throughout.

It's worth spending some time on Harrison Stickle. At 736m it is the highest of the Langdale Pikes and has excellent views. On a clear day Helvellyn, High Street, Kentmere and Black Combe are all in view. It is even said that Ingleborough in the Yorkshire Dales can be seen.

Drop down to the head of Dungeon Ghyll and follow the path to Thorn Crag and Loft Crag, both of which provide tremendous views down Langdale with Windermere in the distance.

To find the next scramble head towards Pike of Stickle. Walk round the base of the familiar cone to the Sticks Pass side. Walk towards Mickleden and look down the scree for a grass platform about 60m further down. Descend the scree, by the edge nearest the rock buttress, to the platform. The short scramble up the west ridge of Pike of Stickle can now be followed at grade 3.

The route is airy and requires a head for heights. It is narrow and quite sustained. Follow a line along a narrow ridge past a series of pinnacles. These also provide adequate belays. The gully on the right falls away steeply and the drop on the left is no less daunting. The top is soon reached and the summit of Pike of Stickle easily gained.

The traverse of the Langdale Pikes now only requires a walk back over to the summit of Pavey Ark. The descent can then be made by Jack's Rake down the cliff-face of Pavey Ark. The top of the scramble is located from the top by finding a cairn by a stone wall to the south-west of the summit. In descent the scramble on Jack's Rake is slightly harder but still only grade 1. Finally descend down the bank of Stickle Ghyll to the start of the day in the Langdale Valley.

# INTRODUCTION TO THE CONISTON FELLS

The Coniston fells capture much of what is best in Lakeland. There are first-rate, high-level, rolling ridge walks and towering cliffs that allow some of the finest rock-climbs in the district. The tarns provide quiet shorelines for a lazy day and some of the valleys remain largely undiscovered by walkers. There are woods and rivers to investigate. Exciting gills and airy ridges offer open invitations to the scrambler. Deep corries and narrow ridges entice any aspiring fell wanderer in to explore further.

The highest of the group is Coniston Old Man. The views from the summit are outstanding. There is a seascape on one side including the Isle of Man and the Furness Peninsula. On the other side the highest fells in England, the Scafell range, line up to be counted. Beneath your feet, on the north-eastern side, there are steep crags sweeping down into tarns and what remains

*The Coniston Fells seen across Coniston Water*

of the copper mines.

Copper has been mined from the Coniston fells since 1599 and possibly before. Production reached its peak in the mid-nineteenth century. The copper was shipped to St Helens in Lancashire where it was used in the manufacturing of wooden ships. The decline in the production of these ships and the discovery of copper mines overseas made the Coniston mines uneconomical, and they eventually closed at the turn of the century.

Apart from Coniston Old Man, the other principal fells are Wetherlam, Swirl How, Dow Crag and Friar's Crag. One of the beauties of these fells is that all these summits can be enjoyed in one 7–8 hour walk. The scrambler can of course vary the route by introducing different scrambles into the approaches. Any of the routes that follow in this chapter can be used to bag all the summits of the Coniston fells.

The most popular approaches are from the Coniston village. The route through the copper-mines valley is a fascinating insight into the past and few people see the remains of the mine-workings as an eyesore. Please note that walkers and scramblers should not be tempted to explore the open mine-shafts in this area. There are many false roofs and hidden tunnels.

As an alternative and less popular approach, there is a route included that begins in the Duddon Valley to the west and a route from Little Langdale to the north-east.

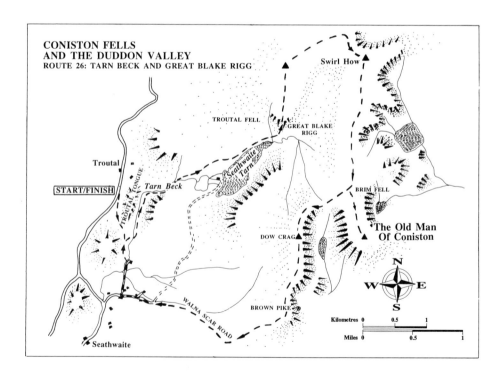

**CONISTON FELLS AND THE DUDDON VALLEY**
**ROUTE 26: TARN BECK AND GREAT BLAKE RIGG**

# TARN BECK AND GREAT BLAKE RIGG

*The unfrequented Duddon Valley holds many secrets. One is the scramble up Tarn Beck which provides a delightful means of gaining the Coniston fells. The scramble over the broken buttress of Great Blake Rigg completes a stunning and secluded approach to the fells.*

*Above Seathwaite Tarn, Duddon Valley, approaching Great Blake Rigg on Grey Friar*

**Grade:** 2/3
**Quality:** ★★
**Distance:** 16km (10 miles)
**Total Ascent:** 830m (2,720ft)
**OS Map:** 90 and 96
**Time:** 6–7 hours
**Start/Finish:** Duddon Valley, at a cattle grid 0.5km south of Troutal (GR 234984)
**Escape Routes:** There are plenty of opportunities to escape from the difficulties. The second scramble over Great Blake Rigg can be bypassed by following a direct path to Lever Hause.
**Notes:** The hardest move of the day is at the start of the grade 3 scramble over Great Blake Rigg. This requires a cool leader and rope protection for the second. Wait for a dry spell. A rope, slings and a selection of nuts are recommended.

A long drive is required to reach the isolated valley of the Duddon. Park at the cattle grid just before Trou-tal. Take the path south-east over Troutal Tongue, crossing a stone wall *en route* to the woods on the river-bank. Swing left at a path junction so that you are walking north along the edge of the river. A path leads along the fringe of the woods where it is necessary to duck to avoid overhanging branches. Cross the river on a wooden bridge to meet a stile. Do not climb this. Instead, trace a line along the stone wall towards the crags on the sky-line. There is no clear path so choose the least soggy bits. The route leads below the crags towards the twin falls of Tarn Beck.

The main two falls lie higher up the fell, but some easy boulder-hopping acts as good training for what is to come. The scrambling begins at the base of twin falls among some trees. At the mouth of these a further waterfall crashes down on the right. There is a ridge ahead with a pinnacle projecting from its crest. Cross the watercourse, then climb up to squeeze behind the pinnacle.

Scramble over rocks to gain the left rocky bank of a narrow watercourse. A slippery boulder provides the key to escape. Climb this on delicate footholds and then step up for handholds above. Pull up and over the edge to the safety of a rocky stance. Water runs down a channel ahead. Step up the side of the wall on the right. This is tremendously exposed with only smeary footholds. Superb flakes of rock on the arête add welcome security for the hands.

At a basin a huge cascade crashes down from the right with a wet boulder hop leading to the base of the main falls. A slippery boulder gives a wet route over the right wall to gain slabs. A jammed boulder on the right wall allows an escape from the grasp of the water and leads to a small platform. Lever over a huge pinnacle to another grass terrace above. Easy scrambling continues to a stream junction. Climb the central series of slabs that take you over the crest of the fell to the base of large waterfalls.

Stay on the left of the falls, passing a small tree at mid-height. The

*Wetherlam from Swirl How*

big waterfall is bypassed on the left while the water spouts from a V-shaped cleft. Easier ground leads to the shore of Seathwaite Tarn. The Coniston fells now arc around the skyline. Craglets cling to the grass and scree slopes but there seem to be no inviting scrambling routes.

To find the continuation of this route, walk along the quiet north shoreline of Seathwaite Tarn. The path continues to climb a steep zig-zagging line to Levers Hause. From the head of Seathwaite Tarn there is more scrambling to be had over Great Blake Rigg, on the lower slopes of Grey Friar. This is the only crag of any significance, and provides an entertaining final climb to the day.

Leave the main path and clamber over boulders to the base of the crag. Start the scramble at a crack around to the right of the lowest point of a prominent nose of rock. To the left there are some large overhangs. The crack is a little too wide to jam your boots into but an arm or leg fits nicely. Climb it from the right then step left across the top of the crack to a platform. This is the hardest part of the grade 3 scramble. Continue up towards a steep face. Follow the rock ramp around to the right in a tremendously exposed position. Good "thank God holds" high up on the right add some welcome security to the situation. Step back left to a huge flake. Either take the exposed traverse on the left around the outside or squeeze through the gap behind the flake for greater security.

A rising traverse from left to right over some rock steps lead to the base of a buttress with a small grass terrace. Walk up more grass terraces trending to the right to a steep rock wall. Pick up the slabs at the base of this wall. Take a line through these just to the left of a grass gully over a series of rock steps to another platform. Follow this to scramble easily up a V-cleft, then clamber over the buttress to another grass terrace where the third buttress lies in wait. The steep face of this buttress is tackled directly over the slabs leading to a steepening, narrow grass ledge. Pick up the fault line leading back to the right and another to a grass platform.

On buttress number four, a V-groove leads up until it is necessary to step left to a small rock platform in an exposed position. The only escape is up, so take the slabs directly over the buttress, trending right then back left. Easier scrambling continues over the top from where a short walk leads to the summit of Grey Friar.

Now that you have gained the tops you can enjoy a leisurely stroll around the fells. Swirl How and Coniston Old Man are well within reach during the afternoon walk. The best descent is to bag Dow Crag then continue down Walna Scar Road to the valley bottom of the Duddon.

# DOW CRAG VIA EASY TERRACE

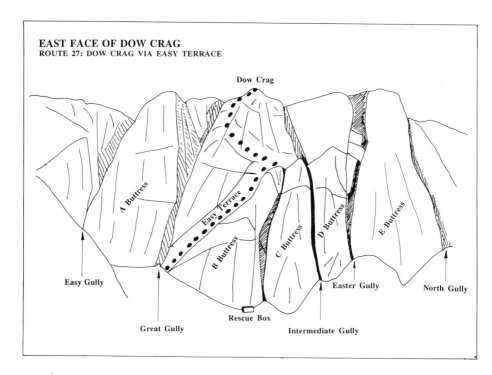

EAST FACE OF DOW CRAG
ROUTE 27: DOW CRAG VIA EASY TERRACE

Dow Crag

A Buttress

Easy Terrace

B Buttress

C Buttress

D Buttress

E Buttress

Easy Gully

Easter Gully

North Gully

Rescue Box

Great Gully

Intermediate Gully

---

*One of the traditional classic lines of the Lake District. The route tackles a weakness across the steep barrier of cliffs that lie on the eastern face of Dow Crag.*

---

**Grade: 3S**
**Quality: ★★**
**Distance: 22km (13 miles)**
**Total Ascent: 1,174m (3,580ft)**
**OS Map: 96**
**Time: 6–7 hours**
**Start/Finish: Coniston village (GR 303976)**
**Escape Routes: The route incorporates the climbers' des-**cent path but this can still be difficult so a rope should be carried to aid an escape. The only escape is to down climb the route.
**Notes:** The scramble passes through steep cliffs where there may be rock-climbers. Wear a helmet, and be careful not to knock any rocks off. Some experience of rock-climbing and the difficulties encountered on big cliffs is desirable. A rope, slings and selection of nuts are recommended.

---

Dow Crag is the name given to the crags and the peak that overlook Goats Water to the west of Coniston Old Man. The Crag is large with excellent rock. The situation is superb, especially once a little height is gained. Climbers have long known Dow Crag and to this day the cliffs are a popular playground. Fortunately Dow Crag is not completely out of the range of the scrambler either, though some climbing experience is desirable. The finest scramble follows the line of Easy Terrace. This is actually part of the descent route for many of the climbs on the Crag but don't be fooled by this; climbers' descent paths can be very difficult, especially with a rucksack and a pair of clumpy boots.

*Walking towards the summit of the Old Man of Coniston*

The usual approach is from Coniston. Climb the steep road beside the Sun Inn which leads on to the Walna Scar road, which is an old pack-horse route. Where the tarmac ends there is a gate that gives entry to a carparking area which is ideal for a shorter round. The Walna Scar road then continues as a rough though mainly level track around the lower southern slopes of Coniston Old Man.

Above Torver Beck, at a huge cairn, there is an obvious path junction. Turn right here, leaving the Walna Scar road to wend its way to the Duddon Valley. The path gradually climbs while Dow Crag comes into view ahead. A final short climb leads to the shore of Goats Water with the cliffs of Dow Crag towering overhead.

Scamper over the boulders around the southern shoreline, then crawl up the scree towards the blue mountain rescue stretcher box at the base of the cliffs. The stretcher box is a useful datum point from which to identify the various buttresses and gullies on the cliffs. The buttresses are named in alphabetical order from left to right. The stretcher box lies below B Buttress.

The scramble begins on the left side of B Buttress just to the right of Great Gully which divides A and B Buttresses. The route climbs diagonally up and to the right on a broad terrace known as Easy Terrace.

Begin at a shallow gully which soon narrows and leads to a rough path. Continue climbing diagonally upwards in the same general line above the steepest cliffs of B Buttress. The path has been well worn

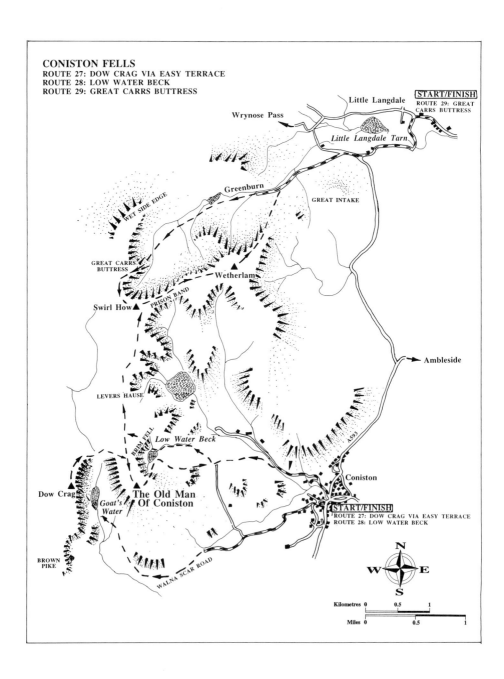

CONISTON FELLS
ROUTE 27: DOW CRAG VIA EASY TERRACE
ROUTE 28: LOW WATER BECK
ROUTE 29: GREAT CARRS BUTTRESS

by climbers descending after a session on the cliff-face. Be careful not to drift off to the right to the tops of the rock-climbs.

Height is quickly gained and the situation is wonderfully spectacular with views out over Coniston Water and to the slopes of Coniston Old Man. The gradient gradually eases towards the top of the terrace as the deep gully known as Intermediate Gully is reached. A route via Intermediate Gully is not recommended due to loose rock, so turn around and retrace a few steps back left. Climb diagonally upwards over blocks and ledges towards Great Gully. This is also part of a climbers' descent route and is therefore well worn. There are some exposed and steep moves so a rope may be required for security. Walk back right to gain the summit of Dow Crag.

Coniston Old Man lies to the east and is now an easy walk away. At its summit the remainder of its satellite fells lie in waiting. Swirl How and Wetherlam can easily be included in the round for the finest circuit. A descent from Wetherlam leads directly back to Coniston village.

*Dow Crag across Goats Water*

# LOW WATER BECK

*Nestled in the lap of Coniston, Low Water has one of the grandest settings in the Lake District. From its shore, Low Water Beck cascades to the Coppermines valley.*

---

**Grade:** 3
**Quality:** ★★★
**Distance:** 9km (5.5 miles)
**Total Ascent:** 750m (2,470ft)
**OS Map:** 96
**Time:** 5–6 hours
**Start/Finish:** Coniston (GR 303976)
**Escape Routes:** Several sections of the scramble are avoidable by sticking to the banks of the beck.
**Notes:** Avoid in high water and when rock is very wet. A rope and selection of nuts and slings should be taken.

---

Many walkers who have followed the tourist path up to Coniston Old Man via Low Water will have noticed the spectacular white foam of Low Water Beck cascading towards the valley bottom. From a distance the falls look impassable, but anyone who has ventured closer will have realised that, though steep in places, there is a route up the side of the falls.

Leave the "old grey village" of Coniston and follow the path signposted "Old Man and Levers Water" beside the Sun Hotel. Later there are signs for the YHA (Coppermines Youth Hostel). The signs lead along the left side of Church Beck across fields and stiles to the disused quarries of Coniston coppermines. A left fork leads steeply towards the summit of the Old Man, but ignore this. Instead, take a right fork towards the Pudding Stone, a huge scoop of rock which provides local climbers with evening sport. Behind the Pudding Stone, you'll catch your first sight of Low Water Beck, crashing down

*Scrambling on the crags of Low Water Beck, Coniston*

*Summit of the Old Man of Coniston, looking over to Brim Fell*

a narrow crevice in the steep rock wall at the rear of the combe.

Start the scramble at the base of the crags where a stream issues from a narrow cleft. Enter this cleft up the right wall of the stream until you are faced with a huge flood of water pouring over a rock shelf. Batten down the hatches to avoid a drenching and escape up the right wall. A safe, dry haven is reached at a grass terrace.

The route now follows the right bank of Low Water Beck, but still with a choice of lines. The most difficult route sticks to the very edge of the beck, with airy views over the cascades in the depths of the ravine, where a slip would be fatal. An easier alternative is to follow the grass terraces to the right. Then turn left and head back to the edges of the beck further up. This option avoids the worst of the difficulties.

Where the two routes meet, the beck has to be crossed. There is a central nose of rock dividing two water chutes. Step across the first watercourse then make an exposed step up on to the central tongue of rock. Fortunately the rock provides wonderful friction, even though the water may be unnervingly washing over the uppers of your boots. Easier scrambling continues up a slab and away from the danger.

The easy progress is short lived and the difficulties return at a steep wall. The water spews from a V-cleft to the right, but there is no way of tracing its course. Instead, climb one of two cracks in the crags to the left. Then walk back to the right to look down on Low Water Beck gushing down a long V-chute in the rock. Climb the easy-angled but narrow arête along the top of the water chute in a very exposed position. Easier scrambling soon leads to the shores of Low Water, tinted by copper deposits.

Ahead, the summit of Coniston Old Man towers above. The best way to continue is to scramble up Brim Fell which provides interesting scrambling at grade 2 from Low Water to Brim Fell.

The scramble begins from the shore of Low Water where a stream issues from a shallow gully over scree. Open buttresses and scree lead to the right from the beck. A fan of scree is reached where it is best to trend to the right to pick up a

ridge with loose pinnacles at its base. Pull carefully on these and scramble up the ridge to a wall. Join the gully on the left before rejoining the ridge once more higher up. The rock improves as height is gained and soon all that remains is a walk to the summit of Brim Fell.

It is now an easy stroll around the tops to Coniston Old Man. A quick return can then be made down the tourist path into the copper-mines valley. Alternatively, for a longer round, walk back over Brim Fell to Swirl How. Descend the Prison Band and head for Wetherlam from where a descent can be made back to Coniston over Furness Fell.

*Scrambling on the crags of Low Water Beck, Coniston*

# GREAT CARRS BUTTRESS

*Little Langdale is the quiet sister of Great Langdale. From it the Greenburn valley creeps up to within scrambling distance of Swirl How. Great Carrs Buttress provides the final adventure on to the popular Coniston summits.*

---

**Grade: 2**
**Quality: \*\***
**Distance: 12km (7.5 miles)**
**Total Ascent: 780m (2,560ft)**
**OS Map: 90**
**Time: 6–7 hours**
**Start/Finish: Three Shires Inn, Little Langdale (GR 315034)**
**Escape Routes: The difficulties can be bypassed throughout for easier options which lower the route to about grade 1.**
**Notes: Generally sound rock. A rope should be carried to allow for some route-finding difficulties.**

---

Park in Little Langdale, to the east of the village along railings. Walk to the Three Shires Inn where you can grab lunch, an evening meal, afternoon tea, bar meals, morning coffee or a traditional pint. Wetherlam, the objective of the day, is clearly in view ahead rising out from the lush meadows of Little Langdale. Swirl How and the crags of Great Carrs can also be identified, though still over an hour's walk away.

Walk down the road, just past the inn, signposted "Tilberthwaite – not recommended for cars". The road descends between stone walls on its way towards the quarries, just poking through the trees ahead. Cross the river via a bridge to enter the edge of National Trust property. Turn right and follow the bank of the river. Walk through a gate and along the track that climbs up and away from the river-bank around the old mines. Another gate is passed and a stile on the right leads down to a footbridge.

*Nearing the end of Great Carrs Buttress, Coniston Fells*

Continue along the main track, passing a small coppice on the right. Follow the path around a white building and climb up into the rough terrain on the edge of the quarries.

At the path junction, take the left fork towards Great Carrs Buttress at the head of Greenburn. The path continues and eventually loses its identity among the bogs near the reservoir. Great Carrs is directly ahead with Swirl How now visible to the left.

A final rise gives a full view of Great Carrs Buttress. Traverse up the left side to gain the beginning of the route which is situated on the side of the crags facing Swirl Hause. Pass a prominent crag on your way, climbing on grass terraces until a large perched block is seen silhouetted against the sky.

You should now be looking at a wide face with a blunt rib of rock rising from the grass, just to the left of a nose. A narrow grass inlet gives access to a rocky rising traverse from right to left with a short problem to begin. Walk across to a steep slab which is climbed to the large perched block seen from the bottom of the route.

You are now on the top of this first section with plenty of options for the rest of the route. The best choice is to head right, over a black mossy area on the side of a rock buttress. This leads over an outcrop. Traverse further right to gain another more continuous ridge which is climbed from right to left. There are plenty of opportunities to alter the line or even bypass the scrambling altogether. Grass terraces divide the rock allowing for plenty of escape routes.

A rocky plateau ahead with scree on the right marks the end of this first section. Walk to the top of the scree then traverse along the top of it to the next spur of continuous rock. If you reach a deep gully you have wandered too far.

The scrambling continues up the left rib of rock that overlooks a gully on the right. At first there are few problems but the route becomes more interesting as height is gained. A number of spikes protrude from the ridge. A grass gully on the left and right provides protection if an escape is required. The ridge finally narrows to an airy traverse of a fine rocky arête to the summit cairn of Great Carrs.

The walk continues around to Swirl How and the Prison Band leading to Wetherlam. All that remains is the steady descent back to Little Langdale via the path over Birk Fell that leads to the mouth of Greenburn.

# WALES

The mountains of Wales are not as popular as those of England. They take more time and effort to discover, but those walkers and climbers who give them a fair chance soon discover their appeal.

Wales has a rich collection of mountains. Some of the most popular lie to the south of the country in the Brecon Beacons where the highest summit, Pen Y Fan, reaches 886m. Here the main summits of the range are noticeably flat-topped with smooth faces and long, broad, grassy ridges. Pen Y Fan, Corn Du and Cribyn are the most frequented mountains as the well-worn paths prove. Unfortunately there is no steep rock of scrambling interest. To find crags, cliffs and ridges for the scrambler, we must head north to the highest mountains in Wales. They are all enclosed in the 2,171 square kilometres of the Snowdonia National Park. There are 14 summits over 3,000ft (914m) in Snowdonia, including Yr Wyddfa, the summit of Snowdon and highest mountain in England and Wales.

The mountains of Snowdonia are mostly rough and rugged. In parts they are smooth and grass-covered but many more have been torn by glaciers to leave mighty cliffs, airy rocky ridges and dark secluded cwms. Walkers' routes to the tops will inevitably climb a steep rocky path or traverse a narrow ridge. The natural progression from walking in Snowdonia is to begin scrambling.

For the scrambler who loves to dance along airy ridges there is no finer place than Snowdonia. Many of the routes are long and most lead to the summit of a 3,000ft peak. The routes are generally more serious than those found in England. A background of mountain-walking and preferably climbing is required to enjoy the scrambles in safety.

The mountains of Snowdonia are collected into groups where long walks can easily cover six mountain summits. There are classic ridge walks and classic rounds to suit everyone. Not surprisingly, perhaps, the scrambler is able to seek out the most remote regions and enjoy solitude, even on a busy weekend in summer when the summits of the Glyders, Snowdon and Carneddau are packed.

The main valley bases are Capel Curig, Ogwen, Llanberis, Beddgelert and Dolgellau.

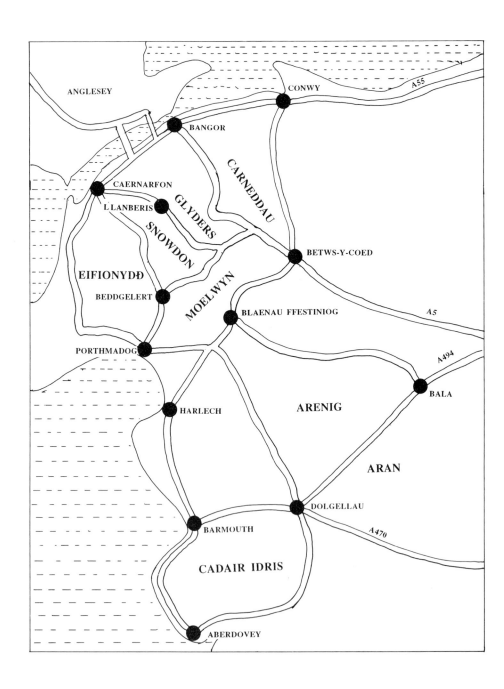

# INTRODUCTION TO THE CARNEDDAU

The great rolling whale-backs to the north of the popular Glyders are the Carneddau. They are the most northerly group of mountains in Snowdonia. There are seven summits over 3,000ft in the range and they provide fine wild and remote hillwalking. Unlike their rocky neighbours to the south, though, they are smooth and generally grass covered. The summits are broad and rounded, with long slender arms between them. Beneath the tops the Ice Age has clawed wild and lonely cwms that are rarely visited. The Carneddau are ideal for long sweeping horseshoe circuits. During good weather you can walk steadily up to the summit plateau and pick off many of the tops throughout the day.

In foul weather, the barren landscape offers no protection from the elements. In winter especially, the Carneddau can be a tough testing place where you need to be well equipped and good at navigation. Many walkers have experienced their first white-out and complete disorientation on these mountains.

The group is bounded by Bangor, Aber and Conway to the north, Bethesda to the west, the Ogwen Valley to the south and the Afon Conwy to the east. The northern tops are rarely visited and offer secluded opportunities for exploration. The most popular summits are Carnedd Dafydd and Carnedd Llewelyn, the highest peak of the group. These mountains lie just to the north of the Ogwen Valley between Bethesda and Capel Curig. They are easily gained from the Ogwen Valley, the most popular starting point for a walk on the Carneddau.

The Ice Age and general erosion have left some crags in the cwms but the best are mainly north-facing and damp. The most popular is Craig yr Ysfa on the Cwm Eigiau shoulder of Carnedd Llewelyn. This has plenty of hard routes and a classic easy rock-climb, Amphitheatre Buttress. Apart from the climbing crags, many others are covered in heather and so the scrambling opportunities are very limited.

The popular circuit of Pen yr Ole Wen by its East Ridge, Carnedd Dafydd and Carnedd Llewelyn does provide some scrambling interest at about grade 1 throughout. But the scrambling is intermittent and of limited duration. This route is also widely documented in various walking guidebooks.

Another famous scramble in the group is the traverse of the pinnacles on the Braich Ty Du Face. Unfortunately the approach to this route is rough and unrewarding. It follows an unstable scree-bed that seems set to tumble into the valley at any time. The final scramble is very short lived, though spectacular, and is followed by a rough walk over heather to the summit.

Undoubtedly the finest scramble in the group is the Llech Ddu Spur above the huge rock face of Crib Lem. This route builds into a superb circuit of Carnedd Dafydd and Carnedd Llewelyn.

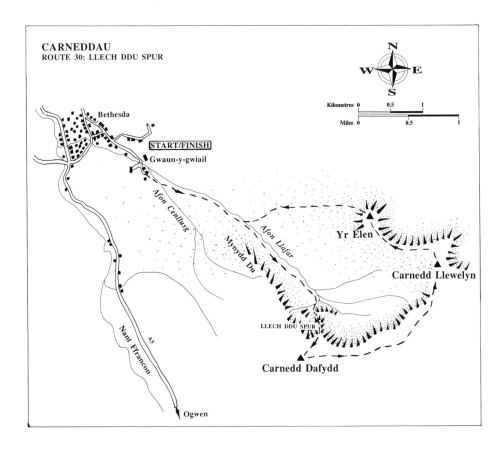

**CARNEDDAU**
ROUTE 30: LLECH DDU SPUR

# LLECH DDU SPUR

*Situated at the head of the secluded valley of Cwm Llafar stands the menacing cliff of Llech Ddu. A long, low-angled ridge leads from the top of the cliff directly to the summit of Carnedd Dafydd.*

**Grade:** 1
**Quality:** ★★★
**Distance:** 13km (8 miles)
**Total Ascent:** 990m (3,250ft)
**OS Map:** 115
**Time:** 6–7 hours
**Start/Finish:** Outside Bethesda at bridge near Water Works (GR 638659)
**Escape Routes:** The difficult sections of the route can be left at many places for the grass terraces that run up the sides of the spur.
**Notes:** There is loose rock in places along the ridge.

*The huge sloping slab on Llech Ddu Spur, Carnedd Dafydd*

There can be few places in Snowdonia that are largely undiscovered by walkers, but the Cwm Llafar Valley is one. It is quiet and secluded and full of crags and gullies to investigate. At the head of the valley there is a huge towering wall of rock overlooking the head waters of Afon Llafar. This is Llech Ddu and, at around 100m high, it is a superb spectacle for the hillwalker and scrambler alike. To find Carneddau's finest scramble the headwall must be bypassed to the right to gain the crest which leads to the summit of Carnedd Dafydd.

Begin the day in Bethesda. If you have a car, leave the busy village by turning right opposite the mountain rescue hut. Continue through the village to a limited parking spot on the corner just before a bridge (GR 638659).

Cross the bridge and turn left up the hill past a house. Climb a stile on the right of the road and walk up the left side of a field to the Water Works. Climb another stile in the left corner of the field behind the

Water Works and follow the faint track up the valley.

Stay on the south bank of the Afon Llafar as you enter the quiet cwm. The path improves and there are superb views back over Bethesda. To the left is the fine conical slate tower of Yr Elan. This will be our route of descent, although from this angle the west face looks dangerously steep. Thankfully there is a good path down it.

Continue along the undulating path on the south-west side of the valley. Ahead you suddenly catch sight of the vertical crags of Llech Ddu with the ridge leading high to the summit of Carnedd Dafydd. Continue along the path until you swing around the corner into the head of Cwm Llafar (GR 666637).

There are huge boulders and scree ahead, leading to the foot of the cliffs. To the right there is the grass ridge of Crib Lem. Our route leads around to the right behind Crib Lem up to a long narrow fall of water. The path is etched into the bed of scree. It is a messy climb but well worth the effort if only for the views across the towering cliffs of Llech Ddu. There are many terraces that tempt the adventurous but leave these and continue behind Crib Lem into Cwmglas Bach.

At almost the level where the gully splits Craig y Cwmglas Bach on the right, a grass ramp leads diagonally back left between bands of rock. Its destination is clear for it leads to the base of the ridge above the dangerous cliffs of Llech Ddu. The grass ramp leads to a bilberry terrace at the base of the ridge. The view is superb for it is undisturbed down the valley over Bethesda to Anglesey.

The scrambling can now begin.

*Walking towards Carnedd Llewelyn from Carnedd Dafydd*

*Scrambling on the Llech Ddu Spur,
Carnedd Dafydd*

At first the route is very vague. Climb steadily over short rock steps and along grass terraces to gain the ground above a rock fin projecting to the sky. Some of the rock is loose, so take care to check your holds. The line continues behind these fins of rock directly on to the crest of the ridge. The ridge is now narrow and grass covered with short rock

pinnacles to test your scrambling skills. Some are too difficult to scramble over while others provide spectacular sport. Large flakes and rocky gullies lead on to a large slanting slab. In wet conditions this would be treacherous, but when dry it provides excellent friction in a most stunning and tranquil setting. To leave the slab there is a long step down.

After a brief grass ridge, there is a section of short climbs and narrow terraces over and around large boulders. A pair of short, narrow, rocky clefts provide bursts of technical scrambling which in turn lead to a final rocky ridge. The high mountains are now only a few minutes' walk away.

Climb the rough scree to the summit of Carnedd Dafydd. The mountain summit marks the end of the climb for the day and is a fine place to take lunch. To descend either walk directly back down the Cwm Llafar ridge, joining the approach path at the head of the cwm. Better still, make a circuit of Cwm Llafar to the summit of Carnedd Llewelyn. This completes the Cwm Llafar Horseshoe, finally descending to the mouth of the cwm via the summit of Yr Elen.

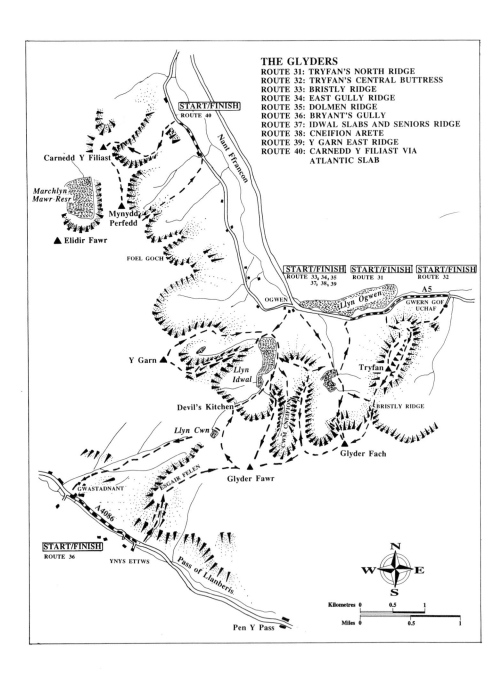

THE GLYDERS
ROUTE 31: TRYFAN'S NORTH RIDGE
ROUTE 32: TRYFAN'S CENTRAL BUTTRESS
ROUTE 33: BRISTLY RIDGE
ROUTE 34: EAST GULLY RIDGE
ROUTE 35: DOLMEN RIDGE
ROUTE 36: BRYANT'S GULLY
ROUTE 37: IDWAL SLABS AND SENIORS RIDGE
ROUTE 38: CNEIFION ARETE
ROUTE 39: Y GARN EAST RIDGE
ROUTE 40: CARNEDD Y FILIAST VIA
          ATLANTIC SLAB

# INTRODUCTION TO THE GLYDERS

Anyone driving down the Ogwen Valley cannot fail to be impressed by the Glyders. The mountains' serrated ridges arc across the sky-line, while rocky secluded cwms lie silently below. There are huge cliffs of rock and waterfalls that cascade into the valley bottoms. The Glyders are sandwiched between the Carneddau to the north and Snowdon to the south. Not surprisingly, they afford stunning views across their neighbours and as far as Moel Siabod and Cadair Idris.

The Glyders extend from Carnedd y Filiast in the north, then stretch south to Glyder Fawr where the ridge swings east to Gallt yr Ogof. Between these extremes lie many of Snowdonia's most famous and finest mountains including the 3,000ft-ers of the group, Tryfan, Glyder Fach, Glyder Fawr and Y Garn. The name 'Glyder' means pile or heap, after the jumble of rocks and boulders that litter these summits.

The mountains are rough and rocky but there are many famous landmarks. The twin square top blocks of Adam and Eve on Tryfan are separated by a gap that is just too wide for an easy stride. There can't be many hillwalkers who

*Y Garn from Tryfan over Llyn Bochlwyd*

haven't made a bold attempt and thankfully succeeded. There is the Cantilever Stone on Glyder Fach projecting out like a spring-board looking ready to topple over at any time. The Castell y Gwent is a strange outcrop of pinnacles between Glyder Fach and Glyder Fawr that adds some scrambling interest to the summit plateau. Finally, there are a multitude of strange rock formations and cairns that become eerie and confusing in the mist.

Below the summits, steep cliffs hug the slopes. These are mainly the home of rock-climbers, but among them there are many classic scrambling routes. Below them huge cwms cradle lakes from where streams roll toward the valley-floor and entice the walker in to investigate.

Walking on these mountains is tough, even by the easiest lines. Most routes will afford some scrambling and many of the most popular ridges, such as the North Ridge of Tryfan and the Bristly Ridge, are pure mountain scrambles. But once height has been gained it is very easy to walk along the rocky plateau picking off tops along the way. It comes as no surprise to discover that among the Glyders are many of the finest mountain scrambles in England and Wales.

The rock is generally very good. There are some loose blocks but most have been removed on the popular routes. Many of the best scrambles lie among the deep cwms and on the rocky ridges that line the northern and eastern faces of the range. The western flank of the Glyders, overlooking the Llanberis Pass, offers plenty of superb rock-climbing but very little for the scrambler except for the classic route up Bryant's Gully to Glyder Fawr. The scrambles are long and committing but memorable. They all lead to a summit and you need to be prepared for a long, tough day in the mountains.

Many of the routes described in this section are on the slopes of Tryfan, Glyder Fawr and Glyder Fach. Most can be reached from a start at Ogwen Cottage or somewhere along the Ogwen Valley.

# TRYFAN'S NORTH RIDGE

*The drive west along the Ogwen Valley is dominated by the serrated profile of Tryfan. From the roadside at Llyn Ogwen the ridge extends at a relentless angle. This ridge provides one of the most entertaining and popular scrambles in Britain.*

---

**Grade:** 1
**Quality:** ★★★
**Distance:** 4km (2.5 miles)
**Total Ascent:** 615m (2,020ft)
**OS Map:** 115
**Time:** 3–4 hours
**Start/Finish:** Park at the lay-by along the A5 below Milestone Buttress (GR 663603)
**Escape Routes:** Most of the difficult sections can be bypassed for steep paths. The route is well polished.
**Notes:** Avoid in wet weather when it is slippery.

---

From the roadside along the A5 at Llyn Ogwen the North Ridge of Tryfan forms an inspiring and spectacular sight. There are crags, gullies and rocky ridges at every turn. Tryfan is a mountaineer's mountain and for the scrambler there are few finer places in the land.

The route up the North Ridge can be varied at will but at first it is safest to follow the line that has been traversed by so many boots over the years. From the lay-by climb a stile and follow the high wall to another stile, which leads to the base of Milestone Buttress. Trend left around this to climb a path up steep scree and a boulder slope. A short barrier at the top gives access to the main ridge. At first, the route direction is difficult to trace. The ridge is wider than expected and there seems to be an endless supply of routes to investigate.

Stay on the left side of the ridge, picking the best line while following

*Scrambling on the South Ridge of Tryfan after reaching the summit by the North Ridge*

the tracks of countless pairs of boots. The scrambling is never technically difficult but there are sometimes route-finding problems. There is a chance to consider your position when the route opens out on to quartz-veined rock.

Walls, gullies and buttresses lead towards the sky as far as you can see. On the west side of the ridge there is a famous landmark known as the Cannon. This huge finger of rock projects from the ridge ready to fire a barrage high over the valley. It marks the halfway point in the scramble. The route continues to the left up more easy scrambling, but don't traverse too far left or else you'll miss the best bits. Another level section leads to a narrower ridge followed by a short notch. A steep 6m descent is required here which will probably prove to be the most difficult section of the route. If you are unsure of this you can detour round it on the left by leaving the crest earlier, approaching the notch from a lower level. This still involves scrambling and, although the difficulty is soon passed, it commands respect as the exposure is quite unnerving. Ascend a gully to the first north

summit. The main summit is a little further on and easily identified by the twin top blocks of Adam and Eve. No one knows which is which.

A complete traverse of Tryfan can be made by descending the South Ridge. This is easier than the North Ridge and is often used as a route to approach the summit of Tryfan via Bwlch Tryfan. In descent the difficulties of the route force the scrambler to the west, and it is necessary to work back round to gain Bwlch Tryfan (GR 659601).

Turn right and follow the Miner's Track down to Cwm Bochlwyd. Follow the path down the west bank of the outflow, recross it again and head diagonally north-east to the A5. Should a shorter round be the order of the day, the North Ridge could be used for a direct scrambling descent. This is not too difficult if the route is known. It is best to follow the path which flanks the North Ridge on its east side.

For those keen on further scrambling, Bristly Ridge lies ahead. This can be gained by following the South Ridge to Bwlch Tryfan from where Bristly Ridge continues on to Glyder Fach.

*View to Blencathra from Clough Head*

*Langdale Pikes from Wansfell*

*Looking up Jack's Rake, Pavey Ark, from the halfway point of the route, Langdale*

*The Cannon on the North Ridge of Tryfan*

*Taking a break by Llyn Bochlwyd.*

*Looking up Bryant's Gully, Glyder Fawr, from near the roadside*

*The Glyders from Y Garn above cloud inversion*

*Looking towards Tryfan and Glyder Fach from Y Garn*

*Snowdon over Llynnau Mymbyr, Capel Curig*

*Descending east towards the main ridge of the Crib Goch traverse*

*Mynydd Mawr with Sentries Ridge on the left*

*Negotiating the Table on the Cyfrwy Arête, Cadair Idris*

*Looking down the Chair of Idris to Llyn y Gadair*

# TRYFAN'S CENTRAL BUTTRESS

*The east face of Tryfan is one of the finest spectacles in Snowdonia. Its main features are the great buttresses divided by deep gullies. This scramble bypasses the steep rock of these buttresses and forces a line up Little and North Gullies.*

**Grade:** 1
**Quality:** ★★
**Distance:** 10km (6 miles)
**Total Ascent:** 615m (2,020ft)
**OS Map:** 115
**Time:** 4–5 hours
**Start/Finish:** Roadside near Gwern Gof Uchaf Farm (GR 673604)
**Escape Routes:** The route can be reversed throughout, but there is no other means of escape.
**Notes:** A well-worn route that provides a quiet alternative to the North Ridge scramble.

The east face of Tryfan exhibits a wealth of rocky buttresses and deep gullies. Much of the face lends itself to low-grade rock-climbing. The best scrambling on the face can be found by following a line up Central Buttress via Little and North Gullies. The route begins on the Heather Terrace and leads directly to Adam and Eve on the summit of Tryfan.

From Gwern Gof Uchaf Farm follow the signposted path that leads around the side of the buildings. Cross a stile and follow the path to the base of Tryfan Bach or Little Tryfan, the huge north-west-facing slanting slab that is easily identified from the road. Trace the path across a boggy area to the fence line across the mouth of Cwm Tryfan. Follow paths to the right and climb a wide scree gully to a plateau with a small cairn. Turn sharp left and pick a line around boulders and through heather to the east face. The path becomes clearer and a broad terrace appears ahead. This is the Heather Terrace and it is from here that many rock-climbs start and our scramble begins. Continue along the path to the first major gully which is deep with large rocks at its base. This is Bastow Gully.

The terrace widens now and you soon reach Nor' Nor' Gully, steeper than the previous one and jammed with large boulders. The next is Green Gully, with grass-covered walls and no obvious continuation below the terrace. This marks the northern extreme of North Buttress. North Gully is the next landmark, being steeper than Green Gully and dividing Central and North Buttresses. About 20m further on, a large boulder splits the terrace. Walk to the boulder and face the cliff.

Leave the terrace by a path on the left that climbs steeply towards the crag, then swing right to gain a grass

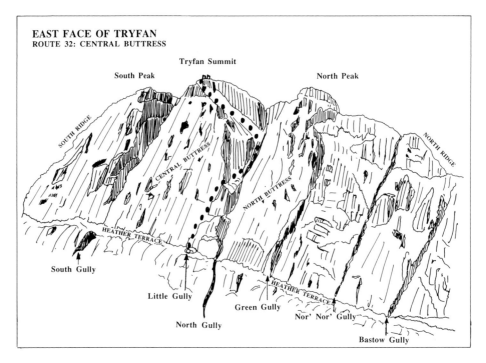

EAST FACE OF TRYFAN
ROUTE 32: CENTRAL BUTTRESS

Tryfan Summit

South Peak

North Peak

SOUTH RIDGE

NORTH RIDGE

CENTRAL BUTTRESS

NORTH BUTTRESS

HEATHER TERRACE

South Gully

Little Gully

HEATHER TERRACE

Green Gully

Nor' Nor' Gully

North Gully

Bastow Gully

plateau above the boulder. Ahead there is a small square-cut gully in the rock wall. This is the end of the walking and the start of the scramble up Little and North Gullies.

Tackle the square-cut gully on its left wall. This is the hardest section of the route, requiring a difficult first step to gain the ledges. The rocky gully continues more easily to a notch overlooking North Gully on the right. There are now large rock slabs on the left and the route continues up the gully to a final rock step. Squeeze between a large over-hanging boulder and the main left wall to reach the end of Little Gully. This is a spectacular viewpoint with the Ogwen Valley stretching out to the east.

A path leads diagonally right from the end of Little Gully to a rock step. Climb the step to reach the rocky bed of North Gully.

Above, the rocks are covered in moss; below, the gully sweeps down to the Heather Terrace. Cross the bed and pick a line up faint zigzags on the right to the mossy rocks. Continue to the end of the gully, with steep cliffs leading to a jagged skyline, and follow a well-worn track for a short distance to the right. At the rear of the amphitheatre is a path junction. Follow the path left across the back of the amphitheatre and pick a line across Central Buttress towards the summit.

There are more rock steps now and the scrambling improves immediately. Some of these are quite committing, requiring care and sure-footedness. To the right you should soon catch sight of Adam and Eve, the two square top blocks on Tryfan's summit. The path winds around the boulders to gain the summit. The best continuation would be to tackle the Bristly Ridge and the Glyders by continuing over the South Ridge to Bwlch Tryfan (GR 662588), eventually descending via Y Gribin or the Devil's Kitchen.

For a shorter round you could follow the North Ridge (Route 31) in reverse. Alternatively, drop directly west from Bwlch Tryfan and follow the path back to the A5 via Cwm Bochlwyd.

*View to the east from halfway up Little and North Gullies, Tryfan*

# BRISTLY RIDGE

*The ridge linking Glyder Fach with Bwlch Tryfan at the end of Tryfan's South Ridge is Bristly Ridge. It is one of the most popular scrambles in Snowdonia.*

---

*Grade:* 1
*Quality:* ★★★
*Distance:* 8km (5 miles)
*Total Ascent:* 760m (2,500ft)
*OS Map:* 115
*Time:* 4–5 hours
*Start/Finish:* **Ogwen (GR 649603). Alternatively, climb Tryfan and descend down the South Ridge to Bwlch Tryfan and continue on to Bristly Ridge.**
*Escape Routes:* **There are many opportunities to bypass the difficult sections.**
*Notes:* **Route-finding can be difficult in the mist. The ridge can be used for a descent with prior knowledge and a rope.**

---

Although Bristly Ridge is only grade 1, it takes the scrambler into superb and often serious situations.

The start of the route at Bwlch Tryfan is best reached after a traverse of Tryfan. If you would prefer to start from Ogwen, leave the roadside and take the path from the carpark that leads behind the toilet block. Fork left and cross a stile and footbridge on to the stone track.

The path curves right to Cwm Idwal, but continue left on to marshy ground. The path leads to the west bank of Nant Bochlwyd and climbs to Llyn Bochlwyd. Cross the stream and continue along the path as it climbs to Bwlch Tryfan (GR 662588).

From Bwlch Tryfan, Bristly Ridge is clearly identified as the pinnacled ridge leading to the south. The scrambling can now begin. It is a little confusing, so check your route carefully.

From Bwlch Tryfan, follow the stone wall to the base of Bristly Ridge. At the lowest crags, walk 10m to the right. Just above an area of quartz veins climb a short gully then escape left over a stone wall. Ahead lies the appropriately named Sinister Gully, long, dark, dank and rugged. Scramble up this, trending on to its left wall as it steepens and becomes difficult to climb. Continue up, then traverse back right to gain easier ground.

A shoulder is reached from where the ridge narrows above. Cross a small pinnacle and continue along to the top of a minor summit, where there are superb views over Llyn Bochlwyd and down the Ogwen Valley to Anglesey. One of the most famous landmarks on the ridge is now ahead – Great Pinnacle Gap, the crux of the route.

Don't get too worried about this section because innumerable pairs of boots have polished the rock,

*The Cantilever on Glyder Fach. This feature is reached soon after the end of Bristly Ridge*

making the route easy to follow. Walk almost to the end of the ridge to overlook the gap. Clamber down a steep step to gain the narrow col. Cross the col then climb a short wall to the right of the Great Pinnacle to a recess behind. Now go through the gap between the squat pinnacle and the main ridge to gain easier ground higher up.

The ridge narrows into a series of pinnacles requiring short descents to avoid the difficulties. This is a superb finale to the route which abruptly ends with easier terrain leading on to the summit plateau. A short diversion to see the Cantilever leads to the top of Glyder Fach.

The best descent from Glyder Fach is to continue over Glyder Fawr to Llyn y Cwm. Follow the outflow of this into the Devil's Kitchen, a huge dark chasm in the rock. From the top of the Devil's Kitchen follow the path to the left which swings down into the head of Cwm Idwal.

To return to the start of the day, continue along the footpath past Idwal Slabs and Llyn Idwal. The path leads directly back to Ogwen.

For a shorter descent follow the scree couloir on the eastern side of Bristly Ridge directly back to Bwlch Tryfan. Retrace the route of ascent back to Ogwen.

# EAST GULLY RIDGE

*A steep ridge scramble over a remote cliff. The route follows a spectacular line over a series of narrow ribs. It negotiates the steep rock above the Alphabet Slabs before emerging on to the summit slopes of Glyder Fach.*

---

**Grade:** 2/3
**Quality:** ★★★
**Distance:** 6.5km (4 miles)
**Total Ascent:** 710m (2,330ft)
**OS Map:** 115
**Time:** 4–5 hours
**Start/Finish:** Ogwen (GR 649603)
**Escape Routes:** The bed of East Gully can be reached at various points along the route. Some sections would be difficult to retreat from without a rope.
**Notes:** The rock dries fast in the afternoon sun. Wait for clear and dry conditions. A rope, slings and selection of nuts are recommended.

---

The huge north-west face of Glyder Fach is an impressive sight. This route takes the most direct and finest line through the difficulties to emerge on to the summit of Glyder Fach. From Llyn Bochlwyd the face is clearly visible. At the middle of its base there is an obvious triangular rock-face. This is the Alphabet Slabs. Immediately to the left of this is Main Gully, while to the right is East Gully. This route climbs the left bounding ridge of East Gully.

Begin the walk from Ogwen. Take the path behind the toilet block towards Llyn Idwal. Where the path swings to the right, leave it and cross marshy ground to gain the path up the side of the stream from Llyn Bochlwyd. Walk around to the east of the llyn, then take a path that swings south-west over boulders and heather into the head of the cwm.

The large triangular Alphabet Slabs should now be clearly in view at the base of the cliff and above a huge bed of scree. The worst section of the day now involves climbing the bed of scree to the base of the slabs.

Start up Main Gully to the left of the Alphabet Slabs for about 30m until a quartz-speckled terrace is reached on the right. Traverse across this to the right above the Alphabet Slabs. A narrow path leads down to a sloping rock platform at the base of a ridge overlooking East Gully.

The scramble now begins with a dizzy traverse around the right of a bulge overlooking East Gully. Fortunately the holds are good and the friction is superb. This leads to a notch behind a block with two ribs and a gully behind. Climb the left rib, or the gully, to gain some steep blocks above.

The scrambling continues

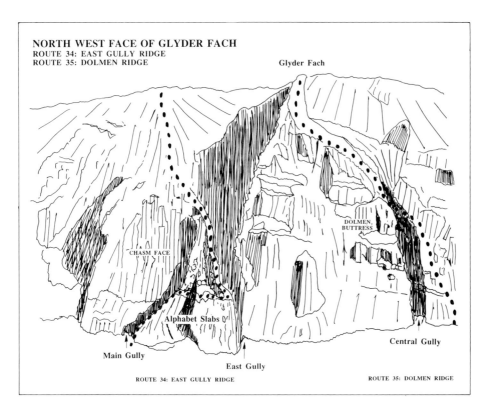

NORTH WEST FACE OF GLYDER FACH
ROUTE 34: EAST GULLY RIDGE
ROUTE 35: DOLMEN RIDGE

Glyder Fach

DOLMEN BUTTRESS

CHASM FACE

Alphabet Slabs

Main Gully

East Gully

Central Gully

ROUTE 34: EAST GULLY RIDGE

ROUTE 35: DOLMEN RIDGE

steeply, overlooking East Gully most of the way until a steepening is reached with a hand-width crack below a smooth rock-face. Climb this with difficulty and mantelshelf or belly-flop on to the top. Alternatively, traverse to the right for about 6m and climb slabs or even join the gully and rejoin the route higher up.

Easy progress continues up the ridge, with a variety of options. Negotiate difficulties on the left or right if necessary, then climb back to gain the crest of the ridge. The ridge eventually swings left to overlook Main Gully then continues left over piles of blocks to join the open rocky slopes of Glyder Fach. The Cantilever Stone is just to the left and the summit rocks are ahead.

To end the round, walk west over Castell y Gwent and descend Y Gribin back to the shore of Llyn Bochlwyd. The main path used for the approach can then be retraced back to Ogwen.

For a longer round, continue over Glyder Fawr and descend the side of the Devil's Kitchen. The path along Llyn Idwal can then be taken back to Ogwen.

# DOLMEN RIDGE

*A long right to left climbing traverse of the north-west cliff-face beneath Glyder Fach, in Cwm Bochlwyd.*

**Grade:** 2/3
**Quality:** ★★★
**Distance:** 6.4km (4 miles)
**Total Ascent:** 710m (2,330ft)
**OS Map:** 115
**Time:** 4–5 hours
**Start/Finish:** Ogwen (GR 649603)
**Escape Routes:** Where the route crosses Main Gully a descent could be made. Generally difficult to escape but possible with a rope.
**Notes:** The rock dries fast in the afternoon sun. It is best to wait for clear and dry conditions. A rope, slings and selection of nuts are recommended.

*Crossing quartz rock at the start of Dolmen Ridge, Glyder Fach*

The huge north-west cliff-face of Glyder Fach is an impressive sight from Llyn Bochlwyd. The rock looks steep and unfriendly, but it holds some of the finest scrambles in England and Wales.

At the foot of the cliffs, towards the middle of the face, there is a distinctive triangular buttress known as the Alphabet Slabs. Immediately to the left of this is Main Gully. A little to the right is East Gully. Much further to the right again is Central Gully (or West Gully, as it is sometimes known). To the left of Central Gully and higher up the cliff-face there is a steep triangular crag. This is Dolmen Buttress. The scramble begins to the right of Central Gully. It then climbs diagonally left and crosses Central Gully at mid-height to gain the ridge above Dolmen Buttress. The rock is steep in places but generally sound. Some tricky moves on the first section lead to some airy moves above Dolmen Buttress.

Begin the day at Ogwen and walk

138

to Llyn Bochlwyd as described in Route 34. Walk around the east side of the llyn towards the back of the upper part of the cwm. Follow a faint path that swings south-west around the end of Llyn Bochlwyd to climb over heather and huge boulders. Walk towards the scree couloir that drops from the col between Castell y Gwent and Gribin Ridge. At a tiny pool (marked on the OS 1:25,000 map only, GR 653586) the line of Central Gully is obvious, rising directly up and slightly left over the cliff. Dolmen Buttress should also be identified halfway up the left of the gully.

It is possible to scramble directly up the gully to Dolmen Buttress, but this is a soul- (and sole-) destroying route. A more worthwhile alternative is to climb the rocks immediately to the right of the Buttress. Better still, make a long traverse from the right that gradually climbs to the Dolmen Buttress.

Start at the base of Central Gully. Walk to the right along a broad terrace that rises across the face above the steep crags. At a quartz-covered, sloping slab step around to the right to gain the end of the terrace. It is now possible to begin the rising traverse back left. Soon another quartz-covered slab is crossed, with a difficult step at its end. The traverse continues over a wide groove that splits the terrace and a short climb up a corner crack.

At Central Gully climb up the rock steps on the right until the scree section of gully can be entered directly to the right of the base of Dolmen Buttress. Walk up the gully to some slabs on the left just before a narrowing. The vertical face of Dolmen Buttress towers over on the left. Climb the steep slabs which rise towards the crest of the Buttress. When the slabs end follow a V-groove towards a jammed boulder. Either squirm beneath the boulder or make an airy step out on the left around the arête.

Continue more easily up the main ridge with some spectacular positions overlooking Central Gully. A small col is reached at the head of Central Gully. Good scrambling leads to the summit of Glyder Fach.

The easiest route of descent is to walk back down Y Gribin Ridge to Llyn Bochlwyd and from there back to Ogwen. Alternatively, a longer round would take in Glyder Fawr with a descent down the Devil's Kitchen.

# BRYANT'S GULLY

*The Llanberis Pass is the centre of rock-climbing in Snowdonia, but for the scrambler there is less choice. Bryant's Gully is the finest scramble along the north side of the pass. The route climbs directly from the roadside for approximately 600m on to the Glyders. This is one of the few quality gully scrambles in Snowdonia.*

---

**Grade:** 2/3
**Quality:** ★★
**Distance:** 7.5km (5 miles)
**Total Ascent:** 830m (2,720ft)
**OS Map:** 115
**Time:** 5–7 hours
**Start/Finish:** **Llanberis Pass road opposite the mountaineering club hut and campsite (GR 624568)**
**Escape Routes:** **It is possible to bypass many sections. Where a jammed boulder block has to be overcome to gain an alcove, the only escape is up a steep and unprotectable wall. It is difficult to retrace your steps out of this alcove once entered.**
**Notes:** **Best left for a dry spell. A rope and selection of nuts and slings will be required.**

---

Begin the day along the Llanberis Pass at the lay-by nearest the mountaineering club hut and campsite beside the Nant Peris village sign. To the right there is the right-angled crag of Dinas Cromlech. To the left is the huge cliff of Carreg Wasted. Ahead, a dark gully can be seen disappearing into the Glyders. Where it disappears trees line its banks and a stream is seen spilling from beneath the green canopy.

Leave the road and follow a diagonal scree path up the western side of the stream course. Trace the line of the stream into the jaws of the gully. Scramble up to a rocky bay where the water cascades from the trees above. Follow the edge of the watercourse until it rolls over a smooth boulder at the head of a bay. Escape by crossing to the left bank. Scramble with difficulty up a smooth, slanting slab. Throw your hand over the top edge while your feet are left scratching for holds. Traverse more easily right to gain the ravine behind the smooth boulder. Already, Llanberis Pass will be fading into the distance.

The scramble follows the line of the gully via a series of steps. At one of these steer left, then traverse right through the watercourse to a rocky platform where there is another short rocky step ahead. A good juggy hold directly beneath the flow of water provides the key, and a step to the left overcomes the problem.

If there has been rain recently you will now be feeling it down the back of your neck. Many of the moves so far will have been of an aquatic nature. Clearly it is best to

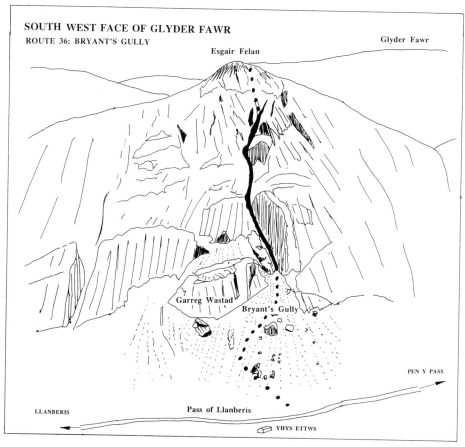

**SOUTH WEST FACE OF GLYDER FAWR**
ROUTE 36: BRYANT'S GULLY

Glyder Fawr

Esgair Felan

Garreg Wastad

Bryant's Gully

PEN Y PASS

LLANBERIS

Pass of Llanberis

YHYS ETTWS

leave Bryant's Gully for a dry spell.

The gully opens out for a short while and is thankfully drier. Easier scrambling leads to a large jammed boulder with water running down its back. Climb the left of this where, if there's a lot of water, you'll get soaked again.

The gully narrows and there is a damp ramp on the right to scramble up. Alternatively, there is an easier escape path further to the right which bypasses the difficulties. At a small amphitheatre there's a narrow water-filled ravine ahead. There is a tricky escape at the end where a rope may be needed to get over the exposed left bank.

Easy scrambling along the watercourse eventually ends at a cul-de-sac with water spouting from a jammed boulder that blocks the passage. There is overhanging rock on the left and a steep grass bank on the right. To proceed over this boulder leads you into serious terrain with no easy escape. Once the boulder has been conquered, the only way out is to climb a steep and loose rocky headwall. This route is unprotectable and demands a very competent grade 3 scrambler. To avoid this danger, escape on a path before the boulder up the steep right wall and rejoin the gully further ahead.

Follow the stream to a second recess where a nasty escape over black rock on the right is required. Easier scrambling then continues up the course of the stream with superb rock scenery throughout. At the head of another alcove with overhanging rock on the left, scramble up right over more black rock to avoid the slimy rocks further ahead. At a dividing riblet with water running over the left wall, take the right fork. Pleasant scram-bling then continues up the rocky, though loose, bed.

Eventually the whole gully opens out on to the red scree below the summit rocks of Esgair Felen. All that remains is to pick a line over the craglets to the summit crest.

Walk over to Glyder Fawr then follow the path north-west to Llyn y Cwm. A path can then be followed all the way back to the Llanberis Pass at Gwastadnant. A short road walk returns you to the start.

*Esgair Felen from across the Pass of Llanberis. Bryant's Gully rises from the centre of the picture*

# IDWAL SLABS AND SENIORS RIDGE

*The huge tilted rock-face of the Idwal Slabs overlooks Llyn Idwal below the northern slopes of Glyder Fawr. They are popular among aspirant rock-climbers, but there is also a superb scramble up their edge that leads to Glyder Fawr.*

---

**Grade:** 2
**Quality:** ★★
**Distance:** 7.5km (4.5 miles)
**Total Ascent:** 710m (2,330ft)
**OS Map:** 115
**Time:** 4–5 hours
**Start/Finish:** Ogwen (GR 649603)
**Escape Routes: The route can be bypassed at various stages, but it would be easy to drift on to more difficult rock.**
**Notes: Some difficult route-finding. The rock dries quickly in the afternoon sun. Avoid in the wet. A rope, slings and selection of nuts should be carried.**

---

The Idwal Slabs aren't marked on the OS 1:25,000 maps, but if you have ever walked to the shore of Llyn Idwal you cannot fail to have noticed them. They are seen as a long clean sweep of slabs rising from the eastern shore of Llyn Idwal.

Above Idwal Slabs is a broken series of short rock walls divided by grass terraces. This is Seniors Ridge. This scramble avoids the steepest sections of Idwal Slabs and takes a line further to the right. It then climbs diagonally right over some small outcrops. Finally, it joins more slabs that lead to the notch in Seniors Ridge above a grass couloir. An easy scramble along Seniors Ridge leads to Glyder Fawr.

From Ogwen follow the main path to Llyn Idwal and continue along the eastern shoreline. Stay on the path as it passes along the bottom edge of Idwal Slabs. On the

*Steep slabs leading to Seniors Ridge above Idwal Slabs, Glyder Fawr*

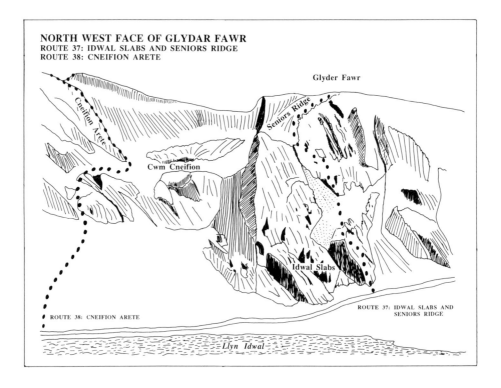

**NORTH WEST FACE OF GLYDAR FAWR**
ROUTE 37: IDWAL SLABS AND SENIORS RIDGE
ROUTE 38: CNEIFION ARETE

Glyder Fawr

Cneifion Arete

Seniors Ridge

Cwm Cneifion

Idwal Slabs

ROUTE 37: IDWAL SLABS AND
SENIORS RIDGE

ROUTE 38: CNEIFION ARETE

Llyn Idwal

right of the buttress there is a deep, dark cleft that separates the main slabs from a subsidiary buttress. Where the path meets the lowest crags of this subsidiary buttress there is a little stream. The scramble begins on the slabs to the left of the stream.

Climb the quartz-faced slabs then trend right as height is gained. The slabs lead to a grass gully. Climb the slabs on the right with steeper slabs further to the right. There are good holds all the way. Where a wide scree gully comes up from below, climb a difficult step up to the left to the summit rocks of the introductory buttress.

High on the skyline is a large notch in Seniors Ridge. A wide, shallow scree and grass gully descends from it. To the right there is a

line of quartz in the rock. The route now heads directly for the right-hand end of this line of quartz.

Begin by clambering easily over small outcrops to the right of the introductory buttress. These lead to a short section of grass which is at the base of the broad couloir that falls from the notch in Seniors Ridge. Climb the slabs on superb holds to the right of the couloir, trending right towards the line of quartz higher above.

At a 15m steep barrier of rock, climb the rib on the right to gain the base of the quartz line. Climb rocks on the right to reach a large tilted table of quartz-covered rock. Walk carefully to the left across the table and pick a line left around crags, along grass terraces and up steep corners towards the notch in Seniors Ridge.

At the notch there is a broad grassy bay. The climb over Seniors Ridge continues to the right. The ridge is broad and scattered with short rocky outcrops, grass terraces and slopes. Pick the best line around the obstacles to reach the summit of Glyder Fawr.

To complete the day follow the main path north-west to Llyn y Cwm. Descend down the sides of the Devil's Kitchen to Ogwen.

*Glyder Fach from Glyder Fawr*

# CNEIFION ARETE

*A long and steep serrated ridge that gives prolonged scrambling to the summit of Glyder Fawr.*

**Grade:** 3S
**Quality:** ★★★
**Distance:** 7.2km (4.5 miles)
**Total Ascent:** 710m (2,330ft)
**OS Map:** 115
**Time:** 4–5 hours
**Start/Finish:** Ogwen (GR 649603)
**Escape Routes: Only by retracing the route, for which a rope would be essential.**
**Notes: A steep and polished route with a difficult start that should be climbed roped-up with running belays. A rope, slings and selection of nuts will be required. Avoid in wet weather or high winds.**

*Scrambling on Cneifion Arête, Glyder Fawr*

The Cneifion Arête is situated on the western flank of the Gribin Ridge and from a distance can be seen to climb up at about 45 degrees like a very steep knife-edge. The route actually follows the arête formed between vertical crags on the right and broken slabs on the left.

The best approach is from Ogwen along the path to Llyn Idwal. Leave the path about half-way along the eastern shoreline and head diagonally up the grassy hill-side to Cwm Cneifion. The summit of Glyder Fawr lies ahead with the shattered ridge of Seniors Ridge to the right and Gribin Ridge to the left. A band of steep mossy rocks extend to the base of the cwm. Above this a steep, sharp, serrated ridge rises to the sky; this is the Cneifion Arête.

The slabby, vegetated front is avoided by taking a rough scree path to the right. At a near vertical side wall it is possible to climb to the crest up a series of polished holds. This is the start of the route, and most parties will need the protection of a rope.

Climb up for 10m on good juggy holds and spikes, trending left to a belay. An exposed step right on good holds leads to a step back left up to another belay. On the right there is a narrow rocky chimney. Climb this to easier ground above, and another belay.

The scrambling eases and continues with a V-groove up the edge of the arête. The best scrambling can be found along the crest. Often there is an easier path nearby.

Once you have been relaxing for a while a little sting in the tail occurs: you are forced on to the knife-edge ridge once again. A narrow corner leads unexpectedly to a square-topped block with a layer of glistening quartz. The ground drops away on all sides, but thankfully a short step takes you to safer terrain.

More airy ridge scrambling continues until suddenly it is all over and you pop out on to the upper slopes of the Gribin Ridge. The grass shoulder leads easily to the steep section of Gribin and a scurry up this takes you to Glyder Fawr.

A final descent can be made down to Llyn y Cwm and the Devil's Kitchen. Ogwen is then an easy walk away.

*Cneifion Arête seen from the mouth of Cwm Cneifion*

# Y GARN EAST RIDGE

*A superb high-level ridge circuit of Y Garn surrounding Cwm Clyd. The scramble builds to an airy crescendo before joining the rounded slopes of the summit plateau.*

---

**Grade: 3**
**Quality: ★★**
**Distance: 5.5km (3.5 miles)**
**Total Ascent: 640m (2,110ft)**
**OS Map: 115**
**Time: 3–4 hours**
**Start/Finish: Ogwen Cottage (GR 649603)**
**Escape Routes: There are no easy escapes from the most difficult sections of the ridge except by retreat. A rope may be needed to escape.**
**Notes: The ridge is narrow near its end and could be very tricky in high winds. There is some loose rock on the ridge. Avoid in the wet. A rope, slings and selection of nuts are recommended.**

---

Cwm Clyd has bitten a huge chunk out of Y Garn's eastern slopes. In its floor Llyn Clyd nestles in the shadow beneath the summit. There are two ridges encircling the cwm. The western ridge provides a rough scree walk to or from the summit of Y Garn. The east ridge is narrow and rocky in its upper section and broad and craggy lower down. This scramble tackles the rough lower slopes of the eastern arm of the cwm then traverses the narrow rocky crest to gain the summit of Y Garn.

Begin the walk from Ogwen Cottage. Follow the path to Llyn Idwal. Cross the footbridge over the outlet and continue on the path around the western shore. Cross the bridge over the stream from Llyn Clyd. Climb the rough ridge to the right which is the lowest extreme of Y Garn's East Ridge. There isn't a best way over the crags, so just pick the easiest line which tends to be on

*Y Garn from the North Ridge of Tryfan*

148

the left. As height is gained there are a few short problems to add interest to the climb. As the broad ridge begins to narrow, a faint path can be joined. This follows the best line around the outcrops. Finally a broad bilberry terrace is reached. To the left there is an obvious triangular face leading to a rocky ridge beyond. This is the start of the real scrambling.

Do not attempt to climb the steep face direct as it soon becomes desperately difficult. Instead, follow a clear path left around the base of the crag, to overlook Cwm Idwal. On the right there is a long rocky gully that climbs to the top of the buttress. Easier ground continues along the crest to a narrow neck with a steep buttress behind. A short step up without many holds gains the neck from where an airy walk crosses it.

At the steep wall move around to the right via a few airy steps to reach a grass bay. A couple of steps left using the top of a flake for handholds leads up to a rocky corner and some huge boulders. Traverse back to the right and make a wild step across a gap with a jammed boulder in a crack as the main hold.

Easier scrambling over a few boulders leads to the main grass slopes of Y Garn. Gain the summit of the mountain by walking around the rim of Cwm Clyd.

The quickest descent is down the right bounding ridge of Cwm Clyd. This leads easily back down to Llyn Idwal and Ogwen Cottage.

*Tryfan (left) and Glyder Fach (right) seen across a cloud inversion from Y Garn*

# CARNEDD Y FILIAST VIA ATLANTIC SLAB

*This route follows the broken edge of a spectacular huge tilted slab for over 200m from the remote Cwm Graianog to the summit of Carnedd y Filiast.*

**Grade:** 3
**Quality:** ★★★
**Distance:** 5km (3 miles)
**Total Ascent:** 600m (1,980ft)
**OS Map:** 115
**Time:** 4–5 hours
**Start/Finish:** The cattle grid south-east of Tai-newyddion farm along the old Nant Ffrancon road (GR 632634)
**Escape Routes:** It is possible to bypass difficult sections by dropping from the crest to either the left or right side. But in some cases this can result in having to traverse even more difficult terrain. The route cannot easily be reversed.
**Notes:** The route should be avoided in the wet when rock is very slippery. A rope and selection of nuts and slings should be carried.

From the summit of Carnedd y Filiast, the most northerly summit of the Glyder range, Atlantic Slab looks spectacular. Its huge face is tilted to the north and gentle waves ripple over its surface. From the valley the slabs look too difficult to climb and many would be forgiven for bypassing them totally.

Many climbers have already discovered the merits of walking in to these distant slabs. There are many low-grade rock-climbs on Atlantic Slab below the summit of Carnedd y Filiast. One of the routes follows the top broken crest of the slab and this is the route described here. It is named simply The Ridge and is given a grade of Moderate in the climbing guides and therefore lies at the top of the scrambling scale.

Begin the day by driving along the old Nant Ffrancon road to the west of Afon Ogwen. There is a cattle grid just to the south-east of Tai-newyddion Farm, with parking space for two or three cars. On the south-east side of the cattle grid there is access to the hills (GR 632634).

Climb up steep bracken to the south of a stream trending to the ridge on the left. A faint path soon appears that can be traced to a break in the fence at the mouth of Cwm Graianog. Avoid walking directly into the cwm and climb the grassy ridge on the left instead. Walk along the ridge until you are above an old sheepfold in the cwm. From this position it is possible to study the layout of the slabs on the opposite side of Cwm Graianog.

There is a fan of large boulders and scree leading down from the lowest crags to a stone wall. Directly above this scree fan is a huge

**EAST FACE OF CARNEDD Y FILIAST**
ROUTE 40: ATLANTIC SLAB

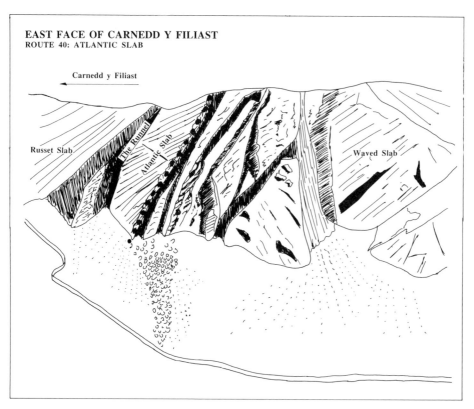

Carnedd y Filiast

Russet Slab

The Runnel

Atlantic Slab

Waved Slab

tilted slab. This is Atlantic Slab; it has a rippled surface with some vegetation and lines of quartz in it. On the left of Atlantic Slab is a gully. This is The Runnel and curves from bottom right to top left around the entire height of Atlantic Slab. Atlantic Slab is also just to the right of a right-angled corner in the stone wall that runs along the base of the slabs.

The route follows the top broken edge of Atlantic Slab. On the left the slab drops to The Runnel, while on the right there are narrow broken slabs and grass gullies.

To reach the scramble, walk across Cwm Graianog over boulders to the stone wall on the other side. Cross the stone wall and follow the large boulder and scree fan towards the base of Atlantic Slab.

Begin the scramble at the lowest point of the slabs on the right. Trend back left and attempt to follow the crest as much as possible. In places it is necessary to step into the bilberry and grass gullies on the right, but sometimes it is easier to stay on the crest itself. It is best to avoid stepping too far left because this will take you on to the slab and this leads quickly on to Difficult-grade rock-climbing.

Climb cracks in the slabs with foot and hand jams. The knee-hold is inevitable and there are a few squeezy clefts to negotiate.

The problems decrease towards the end as the angle eases. A final rocky traverse leads to the summit of Carnedd y Filiast. Walk around the lip of Cwm Graianog to fully appreciate the view of Atlantic Slab.

To continue the walk, head south-east and cross a stile over a wall. It is possible to make a quick exit by walking down the south-bounding ridge of Cwm Graianog, but the finer walk is to continue to Mynydd Perfedd.

Descend steeply to the valley from Bwlch y Brecan. A final walk back along the old Nant Ffrancon road leads to the start of the day.

*View of Atlantic Slab below Carnedd y Filiast*

# INTRODUCTION TO THE SNOWDON RANGE

The first recorded ascent of Snowdon was by the botanist, Thomas Johnson, in 1639. Since that time it has become the most popular mountain in Wales. In 1896 the Snowdon Mountain Railway was completed. This made the mountain accessible to anyone, with the café on the summit providing a comfortable hideaway from the wind and rain.

The highest point of Snowdon is 1,085m and is correctly named Yr Wyddfa, the name Snowdon referring to the mountain as a whole. The summit is often packed to overspill and is definitely not the best place to head for on a bank holiday. Away from the trains, prams and ghetto-blasters, Snowdon is superb. Visit it on a quiet day out of season or descend from it while the sun goes down over Llanberis to see it at its best.

The mountain comprises six ridges that build to a huge pyramid summit. Cwms penetrate every side. Steep cliffs are ideal climbing sport and ridges provide walks and scrambles to the summit. The easiest plod is from Llanberis, alongside the railway, while the most challenging popular route is via Crib Goch from Pen-y-Pass.

The Snowdon group of mountains combine the whale-back grandeur of the Carneddau with the rugged rocky summits of the Glyders. The primary summits are Yr Wyddfa, Crib y Ddysgl, Lliwedd and Crib Goch. The mountains are enclosed by the roads linking Beddgelert, Caernarfon and Pen y Gwryd.

The western side of Snowdon is quiet. The ascents to the tops are long and steady. To the east the Ice Age has bitten deeply into the mountain to create rough rocky ascents. The best scrambles on Snowdon lie here and are easily reached from a base in the Llanberis Pass. Even though Snowdon is littered with crags, only a few make good scrambles as much of the rock is slow drying or too steep to be of interest. But the routes that do exist are superb.

Crib Goch is the most popular scramble in the country and is usually linked with the Snowdon Horseshoe on a circuit from Pen-y-Pass. The hardest route of interest is the Clogwyn y Person Arête that rises from the remote and wild Upper Cwm Glas.

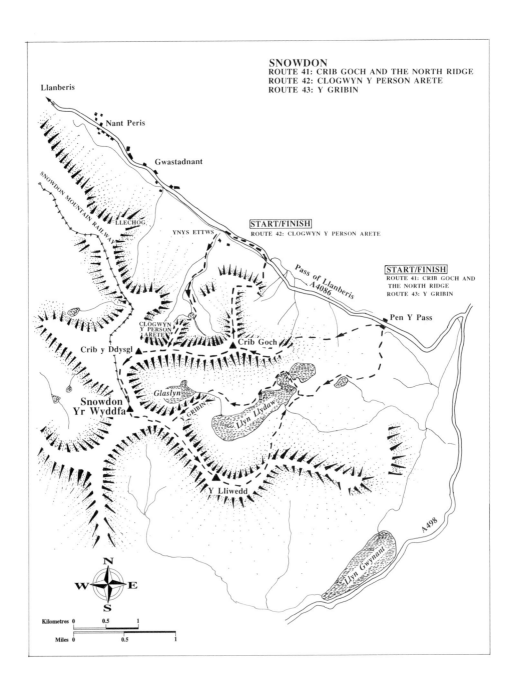

SNOWDON
ROUTE 41: CRIB GOCH AND THE NORTH RIDGE
ROUTE 42: CLOGWYN Y PERSON ARETE
ROUTE 43: Y GRIBIN

# CRIB GOCH AND THE NORTH RIDGE

*Ask people to name a scramble in Wales and the majority will immediately say Crib Goch. It is the most famous and most popular scramble in the country. It is usually combined with an ascent of Snowdon from Pen-y-Pass with a descent over Y Lliwedd to complete the Snowdon Horseshoe.*

---

**Grade:** 1
**Quality:** ★★★
**Distance:** 12km (7.5 miles)
**Total Ascent:** 1,050m (3,450ft)
**OS Map:** 115
**Time:** 6–7 hours
**Start/Finish:** Pen-y-Pass (GR 647557)
**Escape Routes:** It is possible to descend north into Cwm Bach or south on to Glaslyn from Bwlch Coch (GR 621552). The only other means of escape is to retrace your steps.
**Notes:** A popular route that is best left for weekdays. Alternatively, make an early or late start to avoid the crowds. The ridge is best avoided in windy or wet conditions.

---

For many walkers the traverse of this famous pinnacled ridge would have come early in their walking experience. Like Jack's Rake in the Lake District, it has become the route to do and to talk about over a pint in the pub later.

Crib Goch is actually the first peak on the round from Pen-y-Pass and is gained by its East Ridge. The famous pinnacled ridge extends from the summit of Crib Goch to Bwlch Coch, from where the ridge of Crib y Ddysgl continues to the summit of Snowdon.

Begin the day at Pen-y-Pass. A carpark at the top of the pass provides space if you arrive early enough (before 9.30 a.m. on most summer weekends). If there is no space, head down the pass a little to bag a spot in one of the lay-bys.

*High, exposed scrambling on the crest of the Crib Goch traverse*

155

Follow the popular Pyg Track on its way to the Snowdon summit. The track climbs 210m to reach Bwlch y Moch (the pass of the pigs) from where it derives its name. There are good views here over Y Lliwedd and Llyn Llydaw. The Pyg Track crosses the col and contours up above Llyn Llydaw, but our route leads straight up the ridge. Turn right and follow a good path over a shoulder, which provides a very steep rock scramble.

Stay on the ridge, following the polished rock to keep on course. In about 50m the slope eases until the summit of Crib Goch is reached. This is the official summit (921m) though the highest point (923m) lies in the middle of the crest. Ahead, the pinnacled knife-edge ridge of Crib Goch extends towards Snowdon. Once the traverse begins it is best to drop a couple of feet down on the left side towards Llyn Llydaw and use the crest for handholds. Part way along there are the pinnacles of Crib Goch with dramatic views of Llyn Glas and Cwm Glas Mawr.

To negotiate the first pinnacle, drop a little to the left side then scramble back on to the ridge. Take care here not to drop too far down or else you will lose the ridge route completely. Drop to the col between the two pinnacles and continue to the right of the second pinnacle. Scramble over some large steps on exposed rock over the top and down a scree gully to the grass haven of Bwlch Coch.

Follow the path until the broad top of a minor col is reached. Ahead are the huge perpendicular slabs forming the beginning of Crib y Ddysgl of which the highest point is Garnedd Ugain (1,065m). Circumnavigate the rock-face by continuing a little past it on the left side. Scramble back up to the ridge as soon as you can. For the remainder of the ascent of Garnedd Ugain keep to the top of the ridge as much as possible.

Continue over the summit on the path to reach Bwlch Glas which is the crossroads of three major routes on Snowdon. From the north the path rises from Llanberis alongside the railway line, and from the south the Pyg Track rises up the zigzags. Follow the railway for the last 120m to Yr Wyddfa, the highest summit of the Snowdon massif.

The Snowdon Horseshoe continues over Y Lliwedd. From the summit, head south-west a little down to Bwlch Main and a standing stone. Then turn east down the rough, steep path to Bwlch y Saethau and up to Y Lliwedd. Finally, the slow spiral descent to the causeway at Llyn Llydaw and the Miner's Track leads back to Pen-y-Pass.

# CLOGWYN Y PERSON ARETE

*The secluded ridge of Clogwyn y Person Arête provides a remote and challenging climb to the highest mountain in Wales. When combined with a traverse of Crib Goch, it ranks as one of the finest day's scrambling in the country.*

*The final rocky rib on Clogwyn y Person Arête, Snowdon, with the Glyders behind*

**Grade:** 3
**Quality:** ★★★
**Distance:** 5.5km (3.5 miles)
**Total Ascent:** 910km (2,990 ft)
**OS Map:** 115
**Time:** 6–8 hours
**Start/Finish:** Llanberis Pass at Blaen y Nant (GR 623570)
**Escape Routes:** Once the route is started there is no easy escape except by abseil.
**Notes:** This route lies at the top of its grade. There are many route-finding difficulties and there is no singular line to follow. A rope and selection of nuts and slings are recommended. The rock is generally sound but the route should be avoided in the wet.

The Clogwyn y Person Arête lies on the north-east side of Crib y Ddysgl and rises from the compact slab of the Parson's Nose. The route is often quiet because the long approach deters all bar the most dedicated mountain scrambler. For those who make the effort, the route provides an ideal ascent to the Snowdon summit. There is the added bonus of being able to enjoy a quiet descent over Crib Goch in the evening, when the crowds have dispersed.

Begin the day from the Llanberis Pass. There is parking in several lay-bys down the Pass. If you arrive late head for the village of Nant Peris, where there is ample free parking. You will also be faced with a rather long road walk back up the Pass.

Leave the A4086 Llanberis road at Blaen Y Nant (GR 623570). Cross the river on a well-defined path which leads up the west bank of the stream into Cwm Glas Mawr. Extensive views build behind over

*Scrambling on Clogwyn y Person Arête, Crib y Ddysgl*

the Glyders to the north and down the Llanberis Pass. The path crosses the stream and then soon becomes indistinct. Ahead can be seen a watercourse running over steep cliffs. To the left of this is another stream with a lose scree footpath on its right. This is our approach. Pick the best line through the soggy terrain to reach the base of the stream. The path now improves and it is an easier climb. Continue to Llyn Glas, which is easily identified by its little island set to one side, alive with trees and greenery.

Ahead, the line of Clogwyn y Person Arête is clearly visible above the smooth slabs of the Parson's Nose. It will have taken around an hour and a half to get this far, so have a break beside Llyn Glas and enjoy the solitude. If you have reasonably good eyesight you should be able to spot legions of walkers negotiating the airy crest of Crib Goch. By the time you get up there the crowds will have dispersed and you will be alone on Britain's most famous and popular scramble.

Once rested, head directly for the base of the Parson's Nose. A path is joined and this leads around to the west side of the slabs. To climb the slabs direct would be far beyond the means of the scrambler. Our route takes a line up the Western Gully of the Nose. This is mainly on ledges divided by steep and difficult steps. This first section sets the standard for the whole route with the exception that it is possible to escape if necessary. On the remainder of the route there is no means of escape except by abseil or very difficult back-climbing.

The broad spur of Clogwyn y Person Arête now lies before you. The ridge consists of short steps which are divided by broad ledges, adding a minimal sense of security. The ridge could be taken direct but this is very difficult. The easier scrambling follows a far more complicated line through the short rocky steps of the ridge.

From the top of the Western Gully pick the easiest line around the difficult steps. There is a gully on the left which can be joined higher up the ridge, thereby avoiding the most airy sections of the crest. There is no single route of ascent – it is up to the scrambler to seek out and conquer the best line. A rope and selection of nuts and slings are recommended.

Ultimately, as height is gained, the scrambling difficulties ease. The rope can be put away and airy ridge-walking leads to the summit of Crib y Ddysgl.

The main trade route over Crib Goch to the summit of Snowdon is now beneath your boots. To the right the broad path leads to Yr Wyddfa, to the left the traverse of Crib Goch lies in waiting. After the antics of the Clogwyn y Person Arête, Crib Goch will be a far easier affair, and if you have timed it right the ridge may be free of walkers.

To end the round descend by the North Ridge of Crib Goch. This begins with a short, narrow scrambling section before the difficulties disperse and a long steady walk leads down the ridge. From the end of the ridge head east to avoid the steep cliffs of Dinas Mot. A cairned path then takes you back to the road in the Llanberis Pass.

# Y GRIBIN

*A quiet alternative to the popular traverse of Crib Goch from Pen-y-Pass to the summit of Snowdon. It gives good scrambling up a broad ridge in wonderful surroundings beneath the towering north-eastern aspect of Snowdon.*

---

**Grade:** I
**Quality:** ★★
**Distance:** 11km (7 miles)
**Total Ascent:** 725m (2,380ft)
**OS Map:** 115
**Time:** 5–6 hours
**Start/Finish:** Pen-y-Pass (GR 647557)
**Escape Routes: Most difficulties can be bypassed.**
**Notes: A quiet route that avoids the crowds on Crib Goch. It can be used in ascent or descent. Makes a good combination in descent after an ascent of Crib Goch.**

---

Y Gribin below Snowdon (not to be confused with Y Gribin in the Glyders) is a route that is unjustly unpopular. This may be because it doesn't end at a summit itself. A continuation along a second, more broken ridge is required to reach the summit of Snowdon. It is, however, a superb route in both ascent and descent. It looks surprisingly easy from a distance, but closer inspection reveals there are many small rock steps and slabs to negotiate. The ridge is easier than the traverse of the pinnacled ridge of Crib Goch and is comparable to the East Ridge of Crib Goch.

Start from Pen-y-Pass as for the Snowdon Horseshoe. Head south on the Miner's Track along with the tourists over Llyn Llydaw's causeway to the old ruined copper-mine buildings at the stream exit of Glaslyn (GR 619545). Y Gribin is now identifiable as the left-bounding rocky spur leading to a col below the east ridge of Snowdon.

Cross boulders at the stream outflow and traverse grass slopes to the base of the first rocky ridge. There are loose rocks on the left, so ascend slabs on the right of the crest at first. Continue in the same general line sticking to the crest when possible, only stepping off to the left to avoid any difficult sections. Look out for polished rocks to keep on the best line. During the scramble there are superb views across Llyn Glaslyn to Snowdon and to Y Lliwedd but the difficulties end too soon, leading to wishes that this ridge were longer.

At a cairned plateau, traverse to the right to Bwlch y Seathau overlooking Cwm Tregalan. From the bwlch, the Watkin Path can be seen rising diagonally to cross the scree on the south-east face of Snowdon's summit. For the best finish, though, follow the less well-defined path up the East Ridge, overlooking the north-east face and Llyn Glaslyn, directly to the summit.

The best descents from Snowdon are to combine the ascent of Y Gribin with the Miner's Track or Pyg Track. Alternatively, descend directly back over Y Lliwedd or even reverse the traverse of Crib Goch for some real adventure.

*The Y Gribin Ridge seen from Crib y Ddsgyl*

# INTRODUCTION TO THE EIFIONYDD HILLS

If you have spent most of your scrambling days on the Glyders and Snowdon mountains then the Eifionydd hills may seem a rather tame affair, but don't be fooled. The calm exterior of these hills hides many superb crags and for the scrambler there is a route to match the best in Snowdonia.

The landscape of the Eifionydd is softened by forest and is not so obviously scarred by the mining industries. The paths, too, are less well frequented and it is possible to see virtually no one on these hills even on a busy bank holiday.

The scale of the mountains doesn't lend itself to multi-day backpacks, but it is possible to spend time getting to know every intimate detail of these mountains and to stroll along rolling hills in the sun, or to spend the morning on one hill and the afternoon on another. They are littered with interest that would go unseen on the more well-known mountains.

The range includes the Hebog and Nantlle hills. The Hebog hills can be walked in one trip from Beddgelert without difficulty. The main range of hills is covered by the Nantlle Ridge which forms a superb ridge walk to the south-east of the

*The Nantlle Ridge from Mynydd Mawr*

B4418, the Rhyd-Ddu to Nantlle road. This is one of the best walks in Snowdonia, and can be compared to the Bristly Ridge or Snowdon horseshoe for walking quality. The scrambling on the route is easy, short lived and well spaced.

The satellite mountain of the Nantlle Ridge is Mynydd Mawr. It lies on the north side of the valley between the A4085 and the B4418 Nantlle Valley road. A full day's walk cannot be planned around this isolated peak so, while everyone heads for its larger and more famous neighbours, Mynydd Mawr is quiet. The hill is ideal for a quiet and easy day away from the crowds.

The Eifionydd hills offer very little for the scrambler. The rock outcrops that do exist are loose and vegetated. The best scrambling can be found on Mynydd Mawr. The rock there is loose and at best suspect, but on the south-east face there is one classic route known as Sentries Ridge. This is the route described in the following pages.

Access arrangements are more restrictive than in other regions of Snowdonia, so stick to the paths. When in doubt enquire and seek permission locally before setting out.

# SENTRIES RIDGE

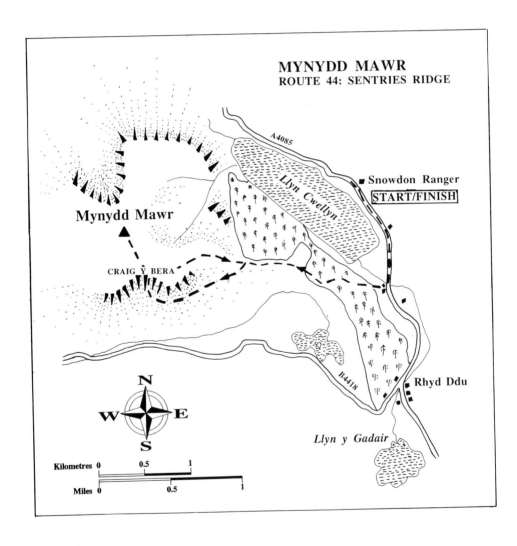

**MYNYDD MAWR**
**ROUTE 44: SENTRIES RIDGE**

A4085

Llyn Cwellyn

Snowdon Ranger
**START/FINISH**

Mynydd Mawr

CRAIG Y BERA

B4418

Rhyd Ddu

Llyn y Gadair

N
W E
S

Kilometres 0  0.5  1

Miles 0  0.5  1

*On the drive north through Rhyd-Ddu the eagle-eyed scrambler cannot help but be drawn to the sight of the ridges on the south side of Mynydd Mawr. There are pinnacles dotted along these slender ridges that assure scrambling adventure. The finest route on the south face is Sentries Ridge.*

---

**Grade:** 3S
**Quality:** ★★★
**Distance:** 9.5km (6 miles)
**Total Ascent:** 550m (1,800ft)
**OS Map:** 115
**Time:** 5–6 hours
**Start/Finish:** Snowdon Ranger Youth Hostel or the carpark to the north-west (GR 565551)
**Escape Routes:** The most difficult section can be avoided by an escape to the gully on the right. There are many opportunities to gain this gully but in some instances this can be very difficult.
**Notes:** There is a lot of loose rock on this route. A rope and selection of nuts and slings are recommended. The route should be climbed roped throughout. Only climb in calm, dry conditions.

---

Sentries Ridge was first climbed by James Merriman Archer Thomson in 1910. Archer Thomson, as he became known, was one of the most noted Welsh rock-climbing pioneers. His first climb was up Deep Ghyll in the Lake District in 1890. He began climbing in Wales in 1894 and raised the standards of gully and face-climbing, especially on Y

Lliwedd. He also wrote the first pocket-sized climbing guidebook to the area. He died suddenly in 1912.

The day begins along the banks of Llyn Cwellyn at the Snowdon Ranger Youth Hostel, or the carpark further up the road if you prefer. Walk back along the road towards Rhyd-Ddu. At the farm near the road bridge (GR 568539) turn right through a gate past the farm. Immediately turn left and climb a stile on to open pasture. Walk diagonally across the field to a gate on the edge of the plantation. Enter the forest and follow a good path diagonally right.

Eventually the path emerges from the forest at a stile. Climb this stile and turn right to walk along the edge of the plantation towards the main ridge of Mynydd Mawr. As height is gained, the views expand to the left down the valley and the Nantlle Ridge.

At the end of the plantation leave the main path and contour left on a faint track below the cliffs. Cross scree then a stile, followed by more scree to the first broken buttress. Ahead can be seen a pinnacled ridge across the skyline. This is not our route, as the main central buttress is far beyond the realms of scrambling. Our route, Sentries Ridge, is to the right of this and set slightly higher up the scree with scree gullies on either side.

Continue on the path over scree passing the first buttress. Turn and face the crags and pick out the line of Sentries Ridge. Clamber over scree and heather to the base of the ridge, where a vertical wall blocks any further progress. Scramble

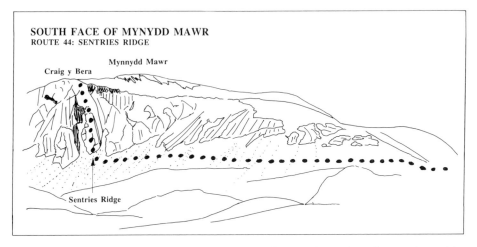

SOUTH FACE OF MYNYDD MAWR
ROUTE 44: SENTRIES RIDGE

Mynnydd Mawr

Craig y Bera

Sentries Ridge

easily up the right on a faint path to gain the top of this first barrier. Pick a line over loose rock and heather, following the crest as much as possible. Take extreme care and consider using a rope to safeguard your ascent.

At a steepening, it becomes very difficult to scramble along the crest. To escape the problems swing left and scramble up loose and moss-covered rock in an exposed position. Belays are possible but check the rock carefully before relying on them. This section finishes at the main pinnacled ridge with a gendarme at its far end.

The traverse of the ridge is the crux and is extremely exposed. If this is not for you, bypass the ridge by simply following a steep path down the right to the gully. You can then return to the crest after about 6m. The traverse of the ridge begins with some extremely airy moves. A rope may be required and is certainly recommended. A couple of slings placed over carefully chosen short pinnacles protect the route but you still need a good head for heights.

Step gingerly along the ridge until you gain the first gendarme. Swing right around this gendarme, placing your boots on a precariously poised sloping block. Fortunately the rock has good friction and there is no difficulty in stepping from it around the gendarme back on to the ridge. The move is made safer by placing a sling just before making the ape-like swing.

Should you wish to escape to the gully on the right, clamber down the rough path on the right. But the scrambling now eases so it is worth sticking to the main ridge.

Continue up the ridge in exposed positions over several pinnacles to a grass col. Once again, this point gives easy access to the gully on the right. It was also here that, in 1910, Archer Thomson originally completed the climb of Sentries Ridge.

The second part of the route follows the broken ridges from the end of Sentries Ridge to gain the summit plateau of Mynydd Mawr. Loose rock and steep sections can be bypassed by entering the gully on the right.

On the final section some shattered gendarmes are best turned on the right to avoid the precipitous slopes on the left. The main path up Mynydd Mawr is now a short walk away.

To descend from the mountain take care to avoid the steep crags and head directly down the main path south-east around the head of Cwm Planwydd. The approach path can then be rejoined at the corner of the plantation.

*The steep cliffs of Craig y Bera on Mynydd Mawr seen from the south*

# INTRODUCTION TO
# CADAIR IDRIS

*Looking west from Penygadair, the summit of Cadair Idris*

Cadair Idris is an impressive mountain range and the most southerly group in the Snowdonia National Park. Its rolling northern cliffs extend for over 11km from Gau Craig, south of Dolgellau, to Craig Cwm-llwyd in the west overlooking the sea. Between these extremes nestle lakes and steep rocky arêtes which give way to low-lying meadows and foothills. There are seven peaks over the 2,000ft (610m) contour in the range, and six of these lie along the northern edge. As would be expected the views are spectacular, especially from the northern

rim, and on a clear day you can see Snowdon.

The name Cadair Idris comes from the corrie basin with Llyn y Gadair nestling in its lap, which is known as the Chair of Idris. The Idris has been depicted as an astronomer, giant, philosopher, poet and warrior. The romance of the name has guaranteed that the mountain remains popular.

In the eighteenth century Robin Edwards of Dolgellau guided tourists over the Cadair Idris range. A stone refreshment building was built on the highest summit, Penygadair, in the early nineteenth century by Dolgellau guide Richard Pugh. Walkers could buy refreshments here while the clouds cleared. Today the refreshments have gone, though the hut remains. It has been rebuilt by the National Park Authority and has wooden benches inside and a corrugated iron roof. It now provides a welcome shelter from the elements.

Fortunately it is still very easy to escape the crowds on Cadair Idris. Cyfrwy, for example, is an excellent vantage-point, but because it lies just to the north of the main route up the mountain it is rarely visited. Or perhaps you could try heading for the extremities of the range where few walkers ever tread.

For the scrambler there is one superb route on the range, the Cyfrwy Arête. This is one of the finest scrambles in the country and offers a unique expedition with airy moves and stunning views throughout. The route lies on the northern escarpment of the main ridge on the edge of the Chair of Idris overlooking Llyn y Gadair. It is ideally approached from a base near Dolgellau.

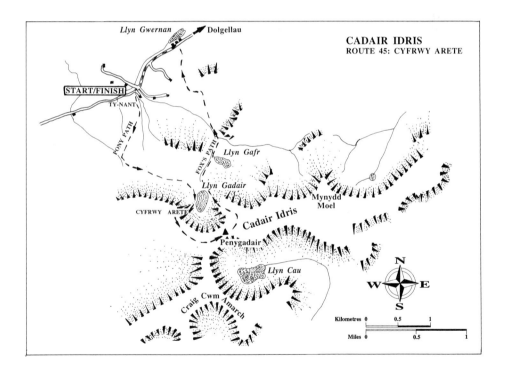

169

*Steep scrambling over loose rock and the pinnacles towards the end of Cwfrwy Arête,*
*Cadair Idris*

# CYFRWY ARETE

*A traditional mountaineering route from the shore of Llyn y Gadair to the summit of Cadair Idris. The notched ridge offers superb airy scrambling with stunning views across Snowdonia.*

**Grade:** 3S
**Quality:** ★★★
**Distance:** 10.5km (6.5 miles)
**Total Ascent:** 890m (2,930ft)
**OS Map:** 124
**Time:** 5–7 hours
**Start/Finish:** Ty-nant carpark (GR 698153)
**Escape Routes:** It is possible to climb down from the sides of the route in a number of places, but a rope would be needed for safety.
**Notes:** The rock becomes very slippery in the wet, so avoid it in such conditions. A rope, slings and selection of nuts are required: the route should be climbed roped throughout. Some sections are very exposed, so avoid the route in high winds.

Owen Glynne Jones, the Victorian rock-climbing pioneer, made his first climb in 1888, on the Cyfrwy Arête on Cadair Idris. He had no nailed boots and climbed it alone without the protection of a rope and without much idea of what he was doing. O.G. Jones went on to discover many new routes and dominated the development of rock climbing in Britain.

The route can be clearly seen from the west at the end of the Cyfrwy cliffs. It lies directly above Llyn y Gadair. There is a flat-topped pillar at just below half height, known as the Table, with a deep notch linking it to the main ridge.

To start the day, park at the Ty-nant carpark (GR 698153). Follow the Pony Path through a gate beside a telephone box. The path leads through Ty-nant buildings where teas, camping and bunkhouse accommodation are available. Pass through a kissing gate to the right of the buildings then follow the bank of the stream towards Rhiw Gwredydd, the col to the west of Cadair Idris summit.

At a stone wall with an iron gate (GR 695143), leave the main path and pick a line leading south-east across soft boggy terrain towards Llyn y Gadair. There is a path but it is difficult to trace. There are good views of the Cyfrwy cliffs on the right and as height is gained the line of the Cyfrwy Arête becomes clear.

Cross a boulder field to reach the shore of Llyn y Gadair. To the north the Cyfrwy Arête rises to the right of a scree couloir. At its base is a large slabby rock-face known as Table Buttress. To the left of this is another rock outcrop. Climb the

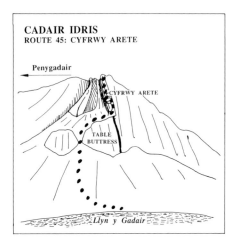

CADAIR IDRIS
ROUTE 45: CYFRWY ARETE

Penygadair

CYFRWY ARETE

TABLE
BUTTRESS

Llyn y Gadair

scree and boulder slopes to gain the bottom of Table Buttress. Then trend left to pick a line around the steep crags and find a scree chute that leads to the top of Table Buttress. Tracks lead above the steep slabs back right to the base of Cyfrwy Arête. The letters "CA" are scratched 50cm high on to a rock to confirm the start of the route.

A rocky arête rises directly above with a groove on the right. Climb the arête on good holds, to a ledge on the right above the groove. Climb a second arête to a corner belay. Walk around to the right to another belay beside some pinnacles. Climb over the crest to gain the edge of the Table, a huge tilted slab speckled with quartz and juggy holds. Crawl or slide down the Table to its lowest corner. Scramble steeply off the end into the notch at the back. Ahead there is a vertical rock-face. Walk to the left and scramble around the corner via a rocky groove to reach a pinnacle with a grassy bay beyond. This is a superb viewpoint, in the shadow of the westerly winds, with Llyn y

Gadair below and the towering wall of Cadair Idris behind.

Scramble directly back to the top of the main ridge via an arête on the right or by a rocky groove to its left. At the top there is a bed of shattered rocks and a stunning view to Snowdon if the weather is kind. After some easy scrambling there is another steepening. Once again the best line lies to the left, this time up an airy arête.

After some more easy moves there is a narrow groove to negotiate. Bridge out on each side and force your way up it to gain the loose boulders above. The most difficult sections are now over. The crest can still be followed and provides some entertaining moves with steep drops on the right.

*The summit of Cyfrwy looking out over Llyn y Gadair*

*Scrambling on Cyfrwy Arête with Llyn y Gadair behind*

The final slopes are easily cracked and the summit of Cyfrwy is close by. It offers panoramic views of Penygadair but is away from the main trade routes of the mountain. Penygadair is only a short walk away to the south-east around the lip of the hollow cradling Llyn y Gadair. The summit trig point stands on a rocky plinth, with the remains of the Victorian ian refreshment hut nearby.

To descend walk north-west from the summit and follow the steep scree path that leads to the shore of Llyn y Gadair. It is then a simple stroll back down the Fox's Path to the road at Llyn Gwernan. A short road walk takes you back to the start of the day at Ty-nant carpark.

# OTHER ROUTES IN ENGLAND AND WALES

Apart from the classic scrambles described in this guidebook there are many more in England and Wales that provide very worthwhile expeditions.

## Howgills and the Yorkshire Dales

### Black Force
Grade: 1
OS Maps: 91, 97 and 98
This scramble follows the bed of Carlin Gill to Black Force. The start of the route is at GR 625995, just east of the M6, which is reached from the north along the A685 road between Kendal and Tebay.

### Ease Gill
Grade: 1
OS Map: 97 and 98
This route provides an entertaining scrambling expedition up the limestone gorge of Ease Gill below the summit of Great Coum in the Yorkshire Dales. Begin the route from Cowen Bridge along the A65 between Ingleton and Kirkby Stephen.

### Swinner Gill
Grade: 1
OS Map: 91
This route is reached along the River Swale from Muker in Swaledale. It climbs along the ledges up the bed of the gill for a short scrambling day.

### Hell Gill
Grade: 1
OS Map: 98
Hell Gill lies along the B6259 just north of Garsdale Head railway station behind Aisgill Moor cottages. The scramble climbs along the gorge beyond the Hell Gill waterfall.

## Lake District
The Lake District is littered with small crags and gills to explore. The best long mountain scrambles have been described in the main text of this book. Other worthwhile routes include the Esk Gorge, in Eskdale, which provides a unique expedition to the Great Moss in Upper Eskdale. Ashness Gill in Borrowdale is excellent for a short and wet scrambling circuit. Blea Water Crag Gill provides a wonderful route to the summit of High Street from Haweswater in Mardale. Finally, Piers Gill can be reached from Wasdale Head and linked with short scrambles over Round How and the ridge leading on to Ill Crags from its North West Combe.

Further detailed descriptions of these, and many more routes, can be found in *Scrambles in the Lake District* and *More Scrambles in the Lake District* by R.B. Evans.

## Snowdonia
The rocky profiles of Snowdonia's mountains provide many opportu-

nities for scrambling. In particular, the east face of Tryfan has a number of excellent routes, including a very good route over the North Buttress and another over the South Buttress. On Snowdon, the Llechog Buttress can be climbed to the Clogwyn station for a superb scramble. A short scramble over the Horned Ridge on the west face of Pen yr Ole above Ogwen is another near classic route, though its interest is sadly restricted to a short section.

Detailed descriptions of these routes and many more can be found in *Scrambles in Snowdonia* by Steve Ashton.

# SCRAMBLING EQUIPMENT AND ROPE TECHNIQUE

Most of the scrambles in this guide could be climbed without a rope and many regard this as the best way to enjoy them. Without a rope there is complete freedom of movement and the scrambler can move quickly over exposed terrain, enjoying the mountains in the most natural way. Remember, though, that the unroped scrambler must not slip. Clearly, the only safe way to do an exposed grade 2 or 3 scramble is as a roped climb, using belays and running belays. The scrambler may only have one hard pitch to climb, but without a rope this may become very serious. To retreat on more difficult routes is often as hard, if not harder, than climbing up the routes.

There is no doubt that the minimal safety equipment of a rope should be carried on all scrambles, particularly routes of grade 2 and above. For much of the route the rope will stay in the rucksack. It may only be used for one short pitch or to safeguard an escape.

However, a rope becomes useless if you do not know how to use it. All the party must understand the basic belaying techniques and how to apply them in a scrambling situation. One member of the party should be an experienced mountaineer who is able to judge accurately when and how to use the rope in various climbing situations.

This appendix explains the basic technical skills and equipment that are needed to safely scramble with a rope. Scramblers should not begin using a rope until they have practised and fully understood the various techniques. The skills can be learned from knowledgeable and experienced friends. It is recommended, however, that scramblers enrol on a course in roped techniques with a qualified instructor.

## Scrambling Equipment

### General Equipment
Scramblers should carry the appropriate map and compass. The best maps for scrambling are the OS Outdoor Leisure 1:25,000 series. These clearly show the crags over which the scrambles lead and are ideal for accurate mountain navigation. Scramblers should also carry a head torch, whistle, a 2.5m × 1.5m polythene survival bag and a basic first-aid kit.

### Clothing
Normal walking clothes are generally suitable for scrambling. The best are those which are close-fitting but allow plenty of freedom of movement. Waterproofs are essential for some of the gill scrambles. Knee-length waterproof jackets are a nuisance, though, and the shorter more technical jackets are a better design for scrambling. Gaiters are worth wearing in gill scrambles,

particularly the type that comple-tely enclose the boot. Gloves should also be carried for belaying to avoid rope burns. Fingerless gloves or tight-fitting thermal gloves are use-ful in cold weather, but require more care when used on difficult scrambles with small holds.

## Rucksack

A neat and narrow close-fitting rucksack is ideal for scrambling. A stabilising waist strap is useful. Avoid rucksacks with side pockets or buckles and straps that may catch on crags.

## Helmets

It is recommended that scramblers wear a helmet. The irritation of wearing one needs to be weighed up against the protection that it offers, both from falling rock and from a blow that may occur during a fall. Helmets are particularly useful in enclosed rocky gullies, where any falling rocks will be funnelled down the gully. The helmet should carry the UIAA (Union Internationale des Associations d'Alpinisme) label of approval.

## Boots

Medium-weight boots with a semi-stiff sole and a narrow welt are ideal. Avoid the very light, bendy boots that are fine for some of the easier scrambles but are useless on more technical routes. Plastic boots and other rigid-soled boots are unneces-sarily clumsy. The boots should have a good sole that grips well on wet rock. The tread pattern should be deep enough so that it doesn't easily clog on muddy terrain or slip on wet grass.

## Rope

The most commonly used rope in a mountaineering situation is a kern-mantle climbing rope with a dyna-mic quality (able to stretch to absorb the energy in a fall). It should carry the UIAA label of approval.

Climbers often use a 45m × 11mm rope. Such a rope can be used for scrambling, but generally it is too long and cumbersome. Some people carry a 15m × 9mm diameter confidence rope. This is light but too short to be of much use in scrambling. The best com-promise is a 36m × 9mm climbing rope. It is also known as a half-rope because it needs to be used double when protecting a leader fall. The 36m length will allow a 15m climb-ing pitch to be climbed in safety, but would be inadequate if used singularly on longer pitches. The rope also allows a 15m abseil during an emergency escape.

Examine your rope regularly for signs of wear. If the sheath is worn through at any point, it should be replaced.

## Other Protective Equipment

An experienced scrambler with a good repertoire of ropework tech-niques will find that most of the scrambles in this book can be ade-quately protected with a rope alone. However, it is often easier and quicker to use some additional equipment.

In general, on grade 3 and some grade 2 scrambles it is useful to carry three or four tape slings with karabiners. Use full strength 25mm-wide pre-stitched tapes. Two of these can be 2.4m long and two 1.2m long. At least two of the karabiners should have a locking screwgate. All should confirm to the latest UIAA standards of approval.

For some of the more technical routes, a small selection of medium-sized nuts (aluminium block attached to a length of wire or cord) should be carried, each with their own karabiner.

If the Italian friction hitch method of belaying is going to be used, a pear-shaped HMS karabiner will also be needed.

## Harnesses

The rope can be tied directly and tightly around the waist. This method is commonly used in scrambling where only a short steep section has to be overcome. Care is needed to check that the rope doesn't ride up beneath the rib-cage where it will cause asphyxiation within ten minutes if hanging free. This method may also damage the internal organs, ribs and spine. Scramblers may prefer to wear a climber's sit-harness, which is very comfortable during a leader fall. However, a scrambler is less likely to take a long fall, except on some more serious routes. A compromise between these two extremes is to wear a climber's belt, which is safer and more comfortable than tying directly on to the rope. It is not as comfortable or as safe as a full sit-harness in a leader fall, though.

## Basic Rope Techniques

Rock-climbers and mountaineers will be able to adapt their normal belaying methods to suit the scrambling terrain and minimal equipment. Hillwalkers will need instruction, ideally from qualified instructors. What follows is an outline of the basic techniques that are required for rope-protected scrambling. The decision of when to get the rope out and use the various rope techniques will depend on such things as the grade of the scramble, the conditions of the rock and the ability and experience of the party.

## Uncoiling the Rope

Resist the temptation to pull the rope out of your rucksack and lay it down on a ledge; it will usually tangle. To uncoil the rope, hold it in one hand, then remove the coils of rope individually and cast them down on the ground in a loose pile.

## Tying in to the Rope

When using a single rope the leader and second should tie in to the end of the rope with a stoppered bowline or stoppered figure-of-eight around the waist (*Fig. 1*). Alternatively, if a climber's belt is used, tie in to that. If a full climber's sit-harness is used, tie in to both the waist belt and leg loops of the harness as per the manufacturer's instructions.

A third member in the party should tie in to the middle of the rope with a figure-of-eight on the bight (*Fig. 1*). This should be connected to the waist belt or harness, if used, via a screwgate karabiner.

If a party has more than three members, the leader and second will climb first. The rope can then be thrown down for other members of the party to tie in to.

If a rope is being used double, the leader should tie in at the middle

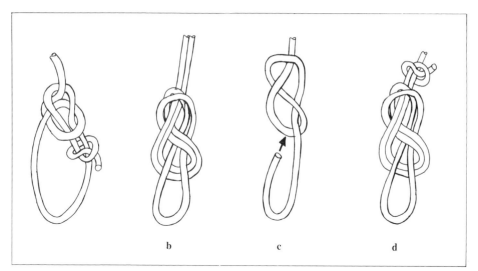

FIGURE 1: SCRAMBLING ROPE KNOTS

*Left to right:*
*(a) Bowline with overhand stopper knot*
*(b) Figure-of-eight knot on the bight*
*(c) Single figure-of-eight knot before rethreading rope back through*
*(d) Figure-of-eight knot with rope threaded back through. Note overhand stopper knot*

with a figure-of-eight on the bight. The second should then tie in to both ends of the rope using stoppered bowlines or stoppered figure-of-eight knots.

## Finding an Anchor

Being tied to the rope is useless if the rope isn't attached to something solid that will not move if you fall. Find a tree, boulder or spike that is solid and definitely not going to move. Remember that it is only this anchor that will hold you in a fall.

The anchor must also be mechanically sound. Try to visualise what will happen during a fall. The rope may pull on the anchor at a different angle than expected – diagonally, vertically or sideways. Will the rope slide off the anchor when pulled? If there is any doubt, find another anchor or attach the rope to two or even three anchors.

Attach the second's rope to the anchor with a figure-of-eight knot on the bight. If the anchor is very tall (such as a tree) the rope needs to be threaded around the anchor then tied back into the main rope at the waist with a stoppered figure-of-eight (*Fig. 1*).

If slings are carried then these can be placed around the anchor (*Fig. 2*). A figure-of-eight knot on the bight is used to attach the rope to the sling via a screwgate karabiner.

Two nuts can also be jammed into cracks to form an anchor (*Fig. 2*). The rope can be attached to one with a figure-of-eight knot on the bight via a screwgate karabiner. The other can be attached using two

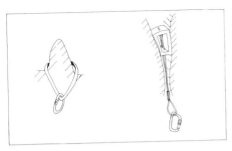

## FIGURE 2: BELAY ANCHORS

*Left: Sling anchor around a rock spike*
*Right: Metal chockstone anchor in a*
*tapering crack*
*Note: A screwgate karabiner is used to*
*link the anchor to the rope*

screwgate karabiners and a sling to the waist.

When using multiple anchors it is vitally important to ensure that all anchors are in tension. If they are not, all the force during a fall will go on to only one of the anchors, in which case it may fail (*Fig. 3*).

## Belaying

Once the second is secure, it is essential that they are positioned in line with the expected pull on the anchors during a fall. The ropes leading to the anchor must also be adjusted so that they are tight. A standing or sitting position can be used and the second must be ready to take a leader fall.

The second's job is to belay (control) the rope while the leader climbs to a ledge above the difficult section. Clearly, the second will be unable to offer much protection during a leader fall. To help compensate for this, some form of friction method needs to be applied that will hold the rope when pulled during a fall. Two methods of

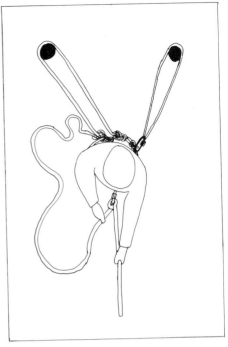

## FIGURE 3: TYING-IN TO BELAY ANCHORS

*A loop of rope has been taken around the left anchor and tied-off at the waist with a figure-of-eight knot. A sling has been placed over the right anchor and clipped to the waist with a screwgate karabiner.*
*Note: the rope and the sling are taut between the belayer and the anchors*

belaying are the waist belay and the Italian friction hitch method.

The waist belay applies a braking force from the friction created between the rope and the belayer's back, hips, arms and hands (*Fig. 4*). The second and more effective method generates braking friction through the Italian friction hitch (*Fig. 5*). This knot is tied around a karabiner at the second's waist (*Fig. 5*).

As the leader climbs, the second

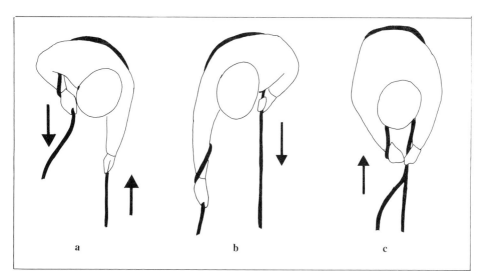

FIGURE 4: THE WAIST BELAY

*(a) The belayer's left hand pulls the live rope which is tied to the scrambler. The belayer's right hand pulls the dead rope forward*
*(b) The belayer's right hand stays forward and holds the rope. The left hand then slides down the live rope*
*(c) The belayer's left hand holds both ropes while the right hand slides back to begin the next cycle. Note: the dead rope is always twisted around the wrist of the dead (braking) hand*

belays until the leader reaches a safe position above the difficulties. The leader then ties in to a safe anchor. Once the leader is secure, the second can release the belayed rope. The leader pulls up any slack rope until it pulls tight on the second. The leader then adopts the belay position. The second may then untie from the anchors when the leader gives the signal. While the second is climbing the leader belays, keeping the rope tight at all times. This will ensure that a fall by the second is arrested almost immediately (*Fig. 6*).

*Communication*
Sometimes it may be difficult to hear or see your climbing partner on

a scramble. On these occasions, and to avoid confusion, a set of calls are used:

**"Safe"** – Leader's call to the second. It indicates that the leader has reached a belay, is secured to an anchor and no longer needs to be belayed by the second. The second may now stop belaying and detach the rope from the belaying device.
**"Taking in"** – Leader's call to the second when about to take in the unused rope.
**"That's me"** – Second's call to the leader when the rope comes tight around the second's waist. The leader then attaches the rope to a belay device and prepares to belay.
**"Climb when ready"** – Leader's

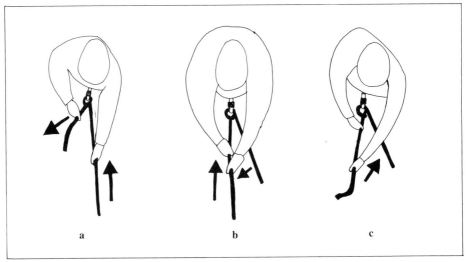

*FIGURE 5: THE ITALIAN FRICTION HITCH BELAY*

*(a) The belayer's left hand pulls the live rope which is tied to the scrambler. The belayer's right hand pulls the dead rope forward*

*(b) The belayer's right hand stays forward and holds the rope. The left hand is crossed over to hold the dead rope above the right hand. The right hand then slides down the rope*

*(c) The belayer's right hand holds the dead rope while the left hand crosses back to the live rope to begin the next cycle*

call to the second. It means the leader has attached the rope to the belay device and the second may start to climb. The leader is now prepared to take a fall from the second. The second may now untie from the anchors.

**"Climbing"** – Second's call to the leader when ready to start climbing.

**"Okay"** – Leader's call to the second to confirm that the second has started climbing and that they are being belayed by the leader.

These additional calls are also useful in some situations:

**"Slack"** – More slack rope is required by a climber.

**"Take in"** – There is too much slack rope for a climber and some should be taken in by the belayer.

**"Tight"** – The climber wants the rope pulled and held tight by the belayer. This term is usually used when a climber is about to fall.

**"Below"** – A loud call to indicate that something, such as rock, is falling to the ground.

The above system of calls provides a security overlap. At any one time, both the leader and the second are anchored to the crag – either by direct anchors or by the belay rope. This overlap should always exist to ensure safe climbing. However, it is easy to forget and inadvertently leave one member of the party not attached to the crag.

Always think when you are

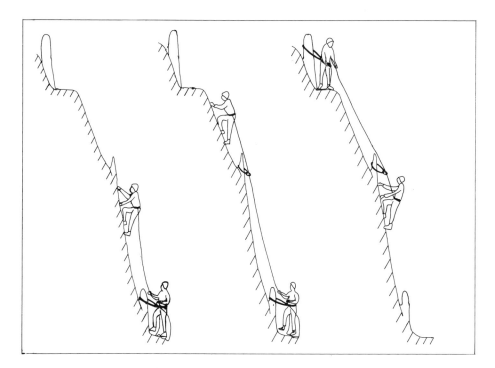

*FIGURE 6: PROCEDURE FOR ROPE-PROTECTED SCRAMBLES*

removing anchors what will happen if you or your second should fall.

*Fixed Runners*

When the leader is climbing he may place additional anchors to shorten the length of a fall. These are called fixed runners. There are many ways of making fixed runners. The simplest method is by placing the rope over a spike or block, which is known as an improvised runner. This is a very quick method which is particularly effective on ridges.

A safer method of providing fixed runners is by placing a sling over a spike which can then be attached to the rope with a kara-biner. Nuts can also be jammed into cracks to provide very secure running belays (*Fig.* 2). When the second climbs up, they detach the rope from the karabiner. The sling or nut can then be removed and carried up to the leader for use on a later section.

Slings are most conveniently carried over the neck and one shoulder. Long slings can be doubled up to shorten them. The karabiner is used to clip both ends together. Nuts should be clipped to a short sling around the head and shoulders or to the waist rope or harness.

Runner placement is an art in itself. Every time a runner is placed it is essential that the force that will pull on a runner will not pull it out. Practise on easy terrain before using these techniques in a dangerous sit-uation. Tuition from a qualified instructor is the best way to learn these skills.

## Moving Together

This technique requires that both the leader and second move along the scramble together. The length of rope between them is shortened and placed over pinnacles while on the move. Moving together is frequently used by alpinists in order to save time. It takes great practice but provides some security, with a minimum loss of speed. It is a system designed for easy terrain when a fall is unlikely. There must be enough belays on the terrain to allow protection to be found quickly and easily. Clearly there is no room for error. Tuition from a qualified instructor is recommended before this technique is used on a scramble.

## Abseiling

If faced with a very difficult pitch that you are unable to climb, it may be necessary to make an escape by abseil. Abseiling needs to be practised in a controlled situation with a safety rope and a qualified instructor. It is difficult to master but may be the only method of retreat. Abseiling relies on basic mechanics with no room for error. It causes more accidents than any other aspect of mountaineering.

If possible, it is often safer to down climb by using the belaying methods described, but in reverse.

## Selecting an Anchor

The quality of an anchor determines the safety of an abseil. Examine the anchor thoroughly to ensure that it is secure. An anchor high above the abseil ledge will prevent the rope rolling off. Check that there are no obstructions that may

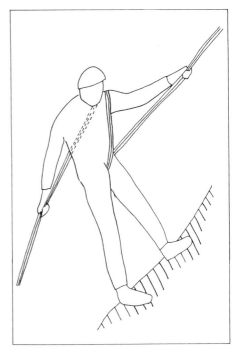

FIGURE 7: THE CLASSIC ABSEIL

jam the rope during retrieval and no sharp edges that may cut through the rope.

It may be necessary to use a taped sling with a karabiner or even, as a last resort, two nuts jammed into cracks as the abseil anchor. If you have to use nuts remember to run the rope through a karabiner to prevent it being cut by the wire trace.

## Abseil Procedure

There are two basic methods of abseiling down a rope. The first is the classic method. This uses no special equipment and requires that the rope is wrapped around the body to provide friction during the descent. It is worth wearing thick clothing to make this more comfortable and to prevent rope burn (*Fig. 7*).

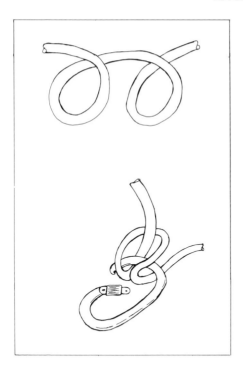

FIGURE 8: THE METHOD OF
TYING AN ITALIAN HITCH ON
TO A SCREWGATE KARABINER

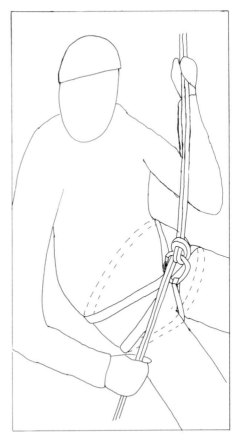

*Abseiling on an Italian Friction Hitch*

The second method is more complicated but more comfortable. If a full sit-harness is not being worn, leg loops need to be improvised from a 2.4m tape sling with the ends linked with a screwgate karabiner. The abseil rope is tied to the karabiner with an Italian friction hitch (*Fig. 8*). The grip on the lower hand controls the speed of descent during the abseil (*Fig. 9*). It is advisable to wear gloves to prevent rope burn.

The rope is attached to an anchor and you are ready to abseil. Tie a figure-of-eight in the two ends of the rope to prevent sliding off the end. Feed the knot down the pitch and check that it reaches the bottom. Walk slowly backwards over the edge while feeding the rope.

Keep the legs well spaced at about hip distance apart, and walk backwards down the crag feeding the rope as you descend. Keep the body almost perpendicular to the rockface to maintain balance.

Once at the bottom, untie the knot in the ends of the rope and pull on one end to retrieve the rope. Watch out for loose stones that may be dislodged.

## Emergency Procedures

It is worth while for every walker to enrol in a basic first-aid course. Here you will learn how to examine a casualty and apply basic lifesaving treatment. Special courses for mountain first-aid are also held by various outdoor centres.

Everyone should learn the basic international distress signal: six successive blasts of a whistle (or torch flashes or shouts) repeated after a one minute pause. The acknowledging response from a rescuer is three blasts of a whistle (or torch flashes or shouts) repeated after a one minute pause. If possible, send someone down to the valley for help, dialling 999 and asking for mountain rescue. The procedure is given in the checklist overleaf.

If the casualty has to be left while you go for help, give them all your spare clothes so they may keep warm. If injuries permit, move the casualty to a sheltered position. Otherwise erect a wind-break around the casualty. Leave the casualty with a torch and whistle to help guide the rescuers. If unconscious, belay the casualty to the rock to prevent a further fall. Mark the position of the casualty with a bright piece of clothing. A rope could be trailed from the casualty to help rescuers trace them.

## First-Aid Checklist

- **Check Breathing**
  If necessary, clear airways with a hooked finger to remove any obstructions.

- **Recovery Position**
  Turn casualty on to the recovery position (unless a spinal injury is suspected).

- **Check for severe bleeding**
  Elevate limb and apply direct pressure to a bleeding wound.

- **Check for broken bones**
  Do not move the casualty if a spinal injury is suspected. Make improvised splints to immobilise other fractures.

- **Monitor condition**
  Keep casualty warm and comfortable while waiting for rescue services.

## Alert Mountain Rescue Team

- Dial 999. Ask operator for mountain rescue service and have the following details written down and ready:

- Number of casualties.

- Names and description of casualties.

- Precise location of casualties including a six-figure grid reference.

- If the casualty lies part way up a cliff, give the name of the route climbed so that rescuers can decide whether to approach from the bottom or top.

- Time and nature of accident.

- Extent of injuries.

- Prevailing weather conditions.

- Remain by the phone until a police officer or member of a mountain rescue team arrives.

## Rescue Helicopters

- Secure all loose equipment before arrival of the helicopter.

- Identify yourself by raising your arms in a V as the helicopter approaches. Do not wave.

- Protect the injured person from the rotor downdraught.

- Allow the winchman to land when ready.

- Do not approach the helicopter unless directed to do so by one of the crew. There are dangers from the rotor and engine exhaust.

# ACCESS AND ACCOMMODATION

## ENGLAND

### Great Gable and Pillar
*Access:* Borrowdale bus from Keswick to Seatoller. B5289 from Keswick to Borrowdale. Wasdale is not served by public transport. From Ambleside, Hardknott Pass and Wrynose Pass lead to Eskdale and Wasdale. Alternatively, A593 Coniston to Torver. At Torver, take a steep right to Ulpha, Eskdale and Wasdale.
*Camping:* Wasdale Head, Seathwaite and Rosthwaite.
*Youth Hostels:* Wasdale and Longthwaite.
*B&Bs/Hotels:* Wasdale Head, Rosthwaite, Stonethwaite and Seatoller.
*Tourist Information:* Seatoller Barn (07687) 77294.

### Scafell Range
*Access:* Lancaster to Carlisle West Coast railway to Ravenglass. The Ravenglass–Eskdale railway runs daily, although very limited service in winter. There is no public transport to Wasdale. Road access as per Great Gable and Pillar.
*Camping:* Wasdale Head and Eskdale.
*Youth Hostels:* Wasdale and Eskdale.
*B&Bs/Hotels:* Wasdale Head and Eskdale.
*Tourist Information:* Cockermouth (0900) 822634.

### Ulpha Fells
*Access:* Regular trains between Lancaster and Carlisle via Ravenglass. Ravenglass–Eskdale railway, although very limited in winter. By road to Eskdale as per Great Gable and Pillar.
*Camping:* Eskdale.
*Youth Hostels:* Eskdale.
*B&Bs/Hotels:* Eskdale.
*Tourist Information:* Cockermouth (0900) 822634.

### Buttermere Fells
*Access:* Train from Penrith or Lancaster to Kendal, then bus to Keswick. The Mountain Goat bus operates a limited service between Keswick and Buttermere. The Borrowdale bus runs from Keswick to Seatoller, where a steep road walk leads to Honister Hause. From A66 west of Keswick, B5292 Braithwaite then Newlands Valley road to Buttermere. B5289 Borrowdale road to Honister.
*Camping:* Buttermere.
*Youth Hostels:* Buttermere and Honister Hause.
*B&Bs/Hotels:* Buttermere.
*Tourist Information:* Cockermouth (0900) 822634.

### Northern Fells
*Access:* Bus service between Penrith and Keswick via Threlkeld. A66 Penrith to Keswick via Threlkeld.

*Camping:* 1.5km south-west of Threlkeld on A66.
*Youth Hostels:* Keswick and Thirlmere.
*B&Bs/Hotels:* Threlkeld, Keswick and Thirlspot.
*Tourist Information:* Keswick (07687) 72803.

## Glaramara
*Access:* Borrowdale bus from Keswick. Short road walk to Seathwaite and Stonethwaite. B5289 from Keswick to Borrowdale.
*Camping:* Seathwaite and Stonethwaite.
*Youth Hostels:* Longthwaite.
*B&Bs/Hotels:* Stonethwaite and Rosthwaite.
*Tourist Information:* Seatoller Barn (07687) 77294.

## Helvellyn and Fairfield Range
*Access:* Bus from Penrith to Patterdale and Glenridding. A592 from Penrith or Windermere to Patterdale and Glenridding. The Kendal to Keswick bus stops at Thirlspot. A591 from Ambleside or Keswick to Thirlmere and St John's in the Vale. No public transport to St John's in the Vale.
*Camping:* Patterdale, Glenridding, St John's in the Vale and Thirlspot.
*Youth Hostels:* Patterdale, Thirlmere, Helvellyn (Green Side), Grasmere (Thorney How and Butterlip How).

*B&Bs/Hotels:* Patterdale, Glenridding, Thirlspot, Grasmere.
*Tourist Information:* Grasmere (05394) 35245.

## Langdale Fells
*Access:* Bus between Kendal and Keswick via Ambleside. Limited buses from Ambleside to Dungeon Ghyll in Great Langdale. From Ambleside A593 to Skelwith Bridge, turning right for Elterwater and Langdale.
*Camping:* Langdale.
*Youth Hostels:* Elterwater.
*B&Bs/Hotels:* Langdale and Elterwater.
*Tourist Information:* Ambleside (05394) 32582.

## Coniston Fells
*Access:* The Coniston Rambler bus from Kendal, Windermere and Ambleside. A591 to Ambleside then A593 to Coniston. No public transport to Seathwaite in Duddon Valley. A593 from Coniston to Torver then go right to Ulpha and Duddon Valley.
*Camping:* Coniston and Seathwaite (Duddon Valley).
*Youth Hostels:* Coniston Coppermines and Coniston Holly How.
*B&Bs/Hotels:* Little Langdale and Coniston.
*Tourist Information:* Coniston (05394) 41533.

## Carneddau

*Access:* Rail and bus between Conwy and Bangor, then Bangor and Betws-y-Coed. Betws-y-Coed to Bethesda buses are very limited outside the peak holidays. A5 Betws-y-Coed to Bethesda.
*Camping:* Capel Curig and some farms in Ogwen Valley.
*Youth Hostels:* Capel Curig and Idwal.
*B&Bs/Hotels:* Capel Curig and Bethesda.
*Tourist Information:* Betws-y-Coed (0690) 710665/710426.

## The Glyders

*Access:* Rail and bus link Conwy, Bangor and Betws-y-Coed. Public transport is very infrequent along Ogwen Valley and Llanberis Pass except during peak holidays. Sherpa buses run in summer. A5 Betws-y-Coed to Bethesda. A4086 Capel Curig to Llanberis.
*Camping:* Pass of Llanberis, Capel Curig and some farms in Ogwen Valley.
*Youth Hostels:* Llanberis, Pen-y-Pass, Capel Curig and Idwal.
*B&Bs/Hotels:* Llanberis, Capel Curig and Bethesda.
*Tourist Information:* Betws-y-Coed, (0690) 710665/710426.

## Snowdon

*Access:* Trains and buses serve Betws-y-Coed. Sherpa buses operate in summer linking Nant Peris and Beddgelert via Pen-y-Gwryd. A5 Betws-y-Coed to Capel Curig. A4086 Capel Curig to Llanberis.
*Camping:* Pass of Llanberis.
*Youth Hostels:* Llanberis, Pen-y-Pass and Bryn Gwynant.
*B&Bs/Hotels:* Llanberis and Beddgelert.
*Tourist Information:* Betws-y-Coed (0690) 710665/710426

## Eifionydd

*Access:* Limited buses between Beddgelert and Caernarfon via Rhyd Ddu. Sherpa bus during the summer. A4085 and B4418 to Rhyd Ddu.
*Camping:* 0.5km north-west of Beddgelert on A4085 and Betws Garmon.
*Youth Hostels:* Snowdon Ranger.
*B&Bs/Hotels:* Beddgelert and Rhyd Ddu.
*Tourist Information:* Betws-y-Coed (0690) 710665/710426

## Cadair Idris

*Access:* Bus to Dolgellau from Porthmadog, Blaenau Ffestiniog, Bala, Welshpool, Cardiff and Bangor. A470 from Blaenau Ffestiniog or Dinas Mawddwy. Signs for Cadair Idris on south-west side of Dolgellau.
*Camping:* Ty-nant bunkhouse and campsite, Kings.
*Youth Hostels:* Kings (Dolgellau) and Corris.
*B&Bs/Hotels:* Dolgellau and Gwernan.
*Tourist Information:* Dolgellau (0341) 422888.

# GLOSSARY OF WELSH PLACE-NAMES

## Pronunciation

Correct pronunciation of Welsh words has always been a problem for non-Welsh speakers. Generally, Welsh words sound as they look, and there are two main differences to English pronunciation. The first is that vowels sound more clipped and pure. Secondly, the stress is on the penultimate syllable. The following short list is a phonetic guide to the main letters that cause difficulty.

### Vowel Sounds

| Short | Long |
|-------|------|
| a : as in hat | a : as in harp |
| e : as in hen | e : as in gale |
| i : as in kin | i : as in been |
| o : as in shop | o : as in more |
| u : as in whim | u : as in clean |
| w : as in foot | w : as in stool |
| y : as in brim | y : as in bean |
| y : as in purse (the words of y and yr sound like this, too) | |

### Consonants

c : as in cot
ch : as in the German *nicht*
dd : as in then
f : as in of
ff : as in off
g : as in get
ng : as in wing
ll : as in l sound but hissed
r : as in English, but trilled
rh : as in English, but more breathy
s : as in sill
si : as in shot
th : as in thing

## Some Common Place-Names

| | |
|---|---|
| aber | river mouth |
| afon | river |
| allt | wooded hillside |
| aran | high place |
| bach | little |
| bala | outlet of lake |
| ban, fan | peak |
| blaen | highland |
| bont, pont | bridge |
| braich | spur, ridge |
| bryn | hill |
| bwlch | col, pass |
| cader, cadair | chair, fortress |
| carn, carnedd | cairn, heap |
| castell | castle |
| cau | hollow |
| carreg | rock |
| cefn | ridge |
| ceunant | ravine |
| clogwyn | cliff |
| coed | wood |
| craig | crag |
| crib | crest |
| cribin | serrated ridge |
| cwm | combe |
| cyrn | peak |
| ddysgl | dish |
| diffwys | precipice |
| din, dinas | fort |
| du, ddu | black |
| dwfr | water |
| dyffryn | valley |
| esgair | ridge |
| fach | small |
| fan | high place |
| fawr | big, great |
| ffordd | road |
| ffridd | hillside pasture |
| ffrwd | waterfall |

| | | | |
|---|---|---|---|
| foel | bare hill | mynydd | mountain |
| gader, gadair | chair, fortress | nant | brook |
| garn | rock | ogof | cave |
| glas | blue, green | pen | top, head |
| glyder | heap | pwll | pool |
| glyn | valley | rhaeadr | waterfall |
| goch, coch | red | rhedyn | bracken |
| gwyn, gwen | white | rhiw | slope, hill |
| gwyrdd | green | rhos | moor |
| gwynt | wind | rhyd | ford |
| hir | long | twll | hole |
| isaf | lowest | ty | house |
| llawr | flat valley floor | tyddyn | cottage, small |
| llech | slate | | farm |
| llyn | lake | | |
| maen | stone | uchaf | highest |
| maes | meadow, field | uwch | above |
| main | narrow | wyddfa | viewpoint, burial |
| mawr | big, great | | mound |
| moch | pigs | y, yr | the, of the |
| moel | bare hill | yn | in |

# BIBLIOGRAPHY

Allen, B., *On High Lakeland Fells*, (Pic Publications, 1988)

Allen, B., *On Foot in Snowdonia* (Michael Joseph Ltd, 1993)

Allen, B., *Escape to the Dales* (Michael Joseph Ltd, 1992)

Ashton, S., *Hill Walking and Scrambling* (The Crowood Press, 1988)

Ashton, S., *The Ridges of Snowdonia* (Cicerone Press, 1989)

Ashton, S., *Classic Walks in Wales* (The Oxford Illustrated Press, 1990)

Ashton, S., *Scrambles in Snowdonia* (Cicerone Press, 1992)

Evans, R.B., *Scrambles in the Lake District* (Cicerone Press, 1988)

Evans R.B., *More Scrambles in the Lake District* (Cicerone Press, 1990)

Fyffe, A. and Peter, I., *The Handbook of Climbing* (Pelham Books, 1990)

Griffin, A.H., *In Mountain Lakeland* (Guardian Press, 1969)

Griffin, A.H., *Adventuring in Lakeland* (Robert Hale Ltd, 1980)

Hankinson, A., *The First Tigers* (Melbecks Books, 1984)

Hankinson, A., *A Century on the Crags* (J.M. Dent & Sons Ltd, 1988)

Hermon, P., *Hillwalking in Wales*, Volumes 1 and 2 (Cicerone Press, 1991)

Marsh, T., *The Lake Mountains* Volumes 1 and 2 (Hodder & Stoughton, 1987)

Marsh, T., *The Mountains of Wales* (Hodder & Stoughton, 1990)

Jones, R., *The Complete Guide to Snowdon* (Gwasg Carreg Gwalch, 1992)

Jones, T. and Milburn, G., *Welsh Rock* (Pic Publications, 1986)

Unsworth, W., *The High Fells of Lakeland* (Cicerone Press, 1992)

# INDEX OF MOUNTAINS AND SCRAMBLES

*Figures in bold indicate illustrations*